Walks in Edinburgh's New Town

The Authors

Michael and Elspeth Wills have been Edinburgh residents for nearly thirty years. Their curiosity about the area's history and its people led them to explore the wynds and closes which lie behind the familiar facades of the Royal Mile. *Walks in Edinburgh's Old Town* was published by the Mercat Press in summer, 1997.

Living and working in the Old Town has not deterred them from making regular forays into the other Edinburgh that lies to the north of the great Princes Street divide. The success of *Walks in Edinburgh's Old Town* encouraged them to discover whether the byways and villages of the New Town could be mapped in the same way into a series of walks for the historically-minded, the Sunday stroller or the simply curious. This book is the result. They are now extending their journeyings to the whole of Scotland as authors of the new edition of *Blue Guide Scotland.*

To Ian and Margaret Gray,
who introduced Elspeth to Edinburgh

Walks in Edinburgh's New Town

Michael and Elspeth Wills

THE MERCAT PRESS

First published in 1998 by Mercat Press
James Thin, 53 South Bridge, Edinburgh EH1 1YS

ISBN 1873644 817

Set in Omega at Mercat Press
Printed and bound in Great Britain by
Bell & Bain Ltd, Glasgow

CONTENTS

LIST OF MAPS

INTRODUCTION

The New Town of Edinburgh is Europe's finest Georgian town centre. It represents a unique coming together of the Classical and the Romantic expressed in townhouse and crescent, church and public monument. It is also a living, changing community, the heart of a great European city. Along with the medieval Old Town, its importance was recognised when the centre of Edinburgh was declared a UNESCO World Heritage Site in 1995.

This guide takes you on ten walks to explore the New Town and the villages on its fringes. Together with its companion volume, *Walks in Edinburgh's Old Town* (Mercat Press, 1997), it covers World Heritage Edinburgh and more besides.

Like *Walks in Edinburgh's Old Town,* the chosen routes lead you away from the traffic and crowds into parts of the city that most visitors and many residents never discover. Although the New Town does not have its counterpart's maze of wynds and closes, there are a surprising number of quiet lanes and paths, picturesque mews, hidden squares and unexpected vistas to set against the elegant Georgian boulevards which most people know as the New Town.

The Walks

Each walk takes you through one or more of the distinctive areas which make up the New Town, exploring its high points and forgotten corners. As a change from the grey of the urban landscape, several walks take in gardens and parkland, old cemeteries, wooded stretches of riverbank or an open summit with views to the sea. You can undertake with R L Stevenson 'many an exploration in obscure corners that are neither town nor country'.

Walks 1 and 2 lead you through the First New Town, best known if least intact. They explore the squares, lanes and mews behind the familiar frontages of the main shopping streets, returning through Princes Street Gardens, the boundary between Old and New Edinburgh.

Walks 3, 4 and 5 survey the later developments: the Second New Town to the north, the Western New Town, and perhaps grandest of all, the Moray Estate in between. Walks 6, 7 and 8 go down into the villages along the Water of Leith. Dean Village and Stockbridge remain distinct communities, while Canonmills and Silvermills have been almost submerged by the expanding city. In Stockbridge you explore the Raeburn Estate, one of the most attractive, if lesser known, extensions of the New Town.

Walk 9 looks for the lost village of Broughton and takes in the top of Leith Walk, while Walk 10 winds round and up Calton Hill with its terraces, views and monumental curiosities.

Since the area covered is significantly larger than that of the Old Town, the walks are rather longer. Each takes an

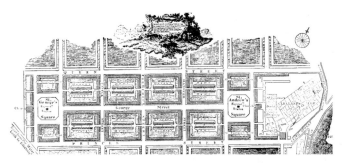

The First New Town

hour to an hour and a half although you can cover the ground in less time or choose to linger longer. The walks are complete in themselves and can be taken in any order. With the aid of the maps, you can even do any given walk backwards. The choice of order and pace is yours.

All the walks are circular, starting and finishing from the same place on Princes Street or at a point easily reached from there. Sketch maps show the route of each walk to help you find your way while the New Town Map shows the area covered by each walk, and how they interconnect, to allow you to pick your own route.

Practicalities

Nothing more than comfortable footwear and provision for the unexpected shower of rain is needed on these urban routes. Stretches of the Water of Leith Walkway can be muddy in wet weather and the stony paths on Calton Hill can be a hazard for those with thin soles and sensitive feet. Edinburgh is a hilly city. This is an essential part of its charm.

Some walks inevitably mean a bit of climbing, although all have long level sections and none are in any way arduous.

Refreshments of all kinds are readily available anywhere in the First and Second New Town, Stockbridge and Broughton. There are, however, sections of Walks 4, 5, 6 and 10 where pubs and cafes are thinner on the ground. There are public conveniences at the Mound, in Waverley Station, in the Gardens at the West End of Princes Street, in the Royal Botanic Garden and by the bridge in Stockbridge.

Edinburgh has a good bus service and almost all go along or cross Princes Street at some point on their route. Information on bus services can be obtained from the Traveline Office at the foot of Cockburn Street, diagonally on your left as you come out the main exit of Waverley Station. Traveline also issues a good bus map. Buses to and from Princes Street to the starting points of walks which do not begin from there are listed in the text.

Open-topped tour buses also take in part of the New Town. Although they are considerably more expensive than the service buses, your ticket is valid for a day and permits you to get on and off at any point on the route. The tour includes a guided commentary to both the Old and New Towns.

The New Town continues to develop. Buildings are repaired and find new uses. While every attempt has been made to ensure that the information given is correct at the time of going to press—summer 1998—inevitably, there will be changes, both temporary and permanent.

Enjoy your walk!

THE DEVELOPMENT OF THE NEW TOWN

'When the New Town began to spread abroad its draughty parallelograms, there was such a flitting, such a change of domicile and dweller as was never excelled in the history of cities.'—R L Stevenson.

Introduction

The New Town of Edinburgh is the world's largest area of classical domestic architecture, covering one and a quarter square miles on a gently sloping ridge above the Firth of Forth. It is a product of the Scottish Enlightenment, that brief period in the late eighteenth century when Edinburgh could rightly claim to be Europe's intellectual capital. Yet at the same time, Scotland, once a proudly independent country, was little more than North Britain, governed by a remote and, to many, alien King and Government, 400 miles away. How all these elements came together to produce a living monument of world heritage stature makes a fascinating story.

Edinburgh in 1750

Edinburgh in 1750 was essentially a medieval city, of high, densely packed tenements or 'lands' ranged along the spine of the High Street and Canongate, the so called 'Royal Mile',

EDINBURGH'S NEW TOWN

WALK 8

WALK 7

WALK 3

WALK 5

WALK 6

WALK 2

WALK 4

NORTH

● starting and ending
point of walk

Overview Map

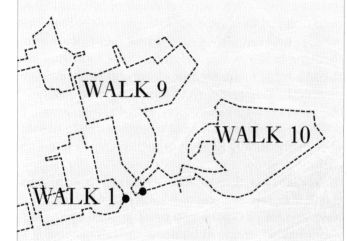

WALK 9

WALK 10

WALK 1

● starting and ending point of walk

though by now Royal only in name. Other than modest suburbs outside the West and Bristo Ports, the city was contained within its medieval confines, bounded by the Flodden Wall to the south and the Nor' Loch to the north.

Unlike most UK cities, Edinburgh had no great river at its heart. The nearest was the Water of Leith, about half a mile north of the Castle rock, at the foot of the slope on which the New Town was to be built. Rising in the Pentland hills, it was, as it is today, little more than a large stream, some eighteen miles long and navigable only at its mouth. Where the river joined the Forth Estuary lay the independent trading port of Leith, over a mile from the capital. In between was open farmland, interrupted only by the rural village of Broughton and a scattering of country houses.

Nonetheless, the Water of Leith was important to industrial Edinburgh as a plentiful source of water to power its mills and for use in the processes of tanning, dyeing and papermaking. Along its banks, a number of small villages had grown up to serve the city on their doorstep.

Nearest the Castle was Water of Leith Village (now Dean Village) at the foot of the gorge. Here were the mills that provided the city with bread. About half a mile to the north east, where the valley widened out, was Stockbridge, the crossing point of the road to the Queen's Ferry, the main route north across the Forth. At Stockbridge a lade ran north of the river, to serve the industrial hamlet of Silvermills before rejoining the river at Canonmills. Here it fed a small loch which powered the mills belonging to the Canons of

Holyrood Abbey, who held the monopoly in supplying the burgh of Canongate with flour.

The city itself had changed little over the previous century. The shock of the triple blow of losing its king and court and then in 1707 its Parliament, was followed by stagnation. Edinburgh kept its head down during the political uncertainty which culminated in the Jacobite rebellions of 1715 and 1745. Sitting not very firmly on the Jacobite fence, it welcomed Bonnie Prince Charlie on his triumphal march with a lack of enthusiasm tempered only by tact.

Although a capital with its heart torn out, Edinburgh still retained a degree of authority, as the seat of an independent Church and of Scotland's separate legal system. Lawyers buzzed round the honey pot of the Court of Session and, increasingly, foreign accents were heard among the students of the University as it acquired an international reputation in philosophy and medicine.

The University was a cornerstone of the remarkable flowering of intellectual life of the period; the hotbed of genius which was the Scottish Enlightenment. Although its richest output—from Adam Smith in economics, David Hume in philosophy, the Adam family in architecture and Joseph Black and William Cullen in science—coincided with the development of the New Town, its seeds lay in the convivial confines of the closes and taverns and in the Old Town's lively social mix. Twenty five years later Mr Amyat, the King's chemist, claimed that at the Mercat Cross he could 'within a few minutes, take fifty men of genius and learning by the hand'.

With the Stuart threat removed, Edinburgh gradually looked to its future. Its more prosperous residents began to compare their small, dark flats where they lived cheek by jowl with all classes of their fellow citizens with the airy squares of neat houses they had seen when visiting London. The comparison was not favourable to Edinburgh.

As early as 1750, new developments were started on the higher ground to the south of the Cowgate, providing some modern housing in Argyle Square, Brown's Square and Adam Square. This was followed in the 1760s by spacious George Square which for a time became much the most fashionable address in town. Edinburgh was at a crossroads. Battered by events, it could sink into provincial stupor or it could adopt the radical thinkers' passion for progress.

Presiding over the city was the all-powerful Town Council, 'omnipotent, corrupt, impenetrable', in Lord Cockburn's memorable phrase. Significantly, it had in its pocket one of the city's major landowners, the wealthy Heriot's Trust, whose membership was packed in the Council's favour. That Edinburgh took the route of progress was down to the vision of one man, George Drummond. He wanted more than the piecemeal expansion of the city to the south. He dared to think the unthinkable: to create a completely new town to the north. Fortunately for future generations, he was the city's boss, its Lord Provost.

Planning the New Town

Expansion of the city northwards was blocked by the malodorous swamp of the Nor' Loch separating the Castle ridge

George Drummond, Lord Provost

from the farmland of Barebones Parks. In 1752, proposals were put forward to bridge and drain the intervening valley and promote a New Town on the Parks. With single-minded zeal, Drummond masterminded the proposals through the Town Council committees and cabals.

By the time North Bridge was completed in 1772, the radically simple plan of the young architect, James Craig, had been adopted. The New Town, based on his concept of two squares joined by three parallel streets along the ridge, was progressing steadily westward.

This, the First New Town, was developed by the Town Council using the process of feuing, a peculiarly Scottish legal device. The landlord granted the developer or feuar an indefinite lease of land in return for an annual payment of feu duty, and subject to whatever conditions the landlord saw fit.

At first, these conditions were far from onerous. The Town Council did not wish to jeopardise its scheme by deterring potential investors. With success came confidence. By the time Charlotte Square was under consideration, anyone wishing to build a house was required to adopt the design of facade which the Council had commissioned from Robert Adam. Charlotte Square established the model for the future, with the landlord commissioning an overall design which individual feuars were then obliged to follow.

By 1800, the First New Town was substantially complete and a proven success. The exodus from the Old Town was fast gaining momentum. Where the Town Council had led, private enterprise was not slow to follow. The owners of the surrounding land wanted a slice of the action. Early in the new century, the Second New Town was laid out, on a similar though somewhat less regular plan, on the downwards slope to the north.

With the end of the Napoleonic War in 1815, the pace of development quickened. Estates were laid out to the west of the First New Town and even across the river, where the painter Henry Raeburn promoted the development of his land near the village of Stockbridge. The building of Regent Bridge in 1821 took the New Town east of Princes Street and released the potential of Calton Hill. Here, a less formal style was adopted, taking account of the contours of the land and giving views precedence over strict geometry. Playfair's proposals for the largest New Town of all, between Calton Hill and Leith, proved a step too far. Only a small part was ever built.

Last but not least, in 1822 the Earl of Moray developed his estate, a strip of land along the Water of Leith to the north west of Charlotte Square. He made full use of his

feudal powers, insisting that buyers pay for all the infra-
structure costs of laying streets and drains as well as adher-
ing rigidly to his designs. Despite, or perhaps because of
the strictness of the conditions, his was one of the most
successful schemes, both commercially and aesthetically.
He himself did very little to further the development but
sat back and enjoyed the profits.

By 1850, the New Town as we know it today was largely
complete. The population of its parish of St Cuthbert's was
nearly 82,500 compared with 57,000 for the whole of the
city a century before. The Town Council was virtually bankrupt and investment money had turned to more profitable
or exciting ventures, notably the railways. Most of the later
developments, including much of the West End and the
Learmonth Estate, were slower to take off and to finish and
had a higher casualty rate. Bankruptcy among speculative
builders was high. Especially on the fringes of the New
Town, incomplete terraces and isolated blocks of grandeur
bear witness to high risks and unfulfilled dreams.

The New Town went through its last but one expansion as
the nineteenth century drew to a close. By now, comfort and
value for money were more important considerations than
elegance. With their bay windows and porches, the terraces
and crescents of Drumsheugh and Coates are solid, confident
and conventional. The New Town was no longer new but an
accepted part of the fabric of a rapidly expanding city.

Today, as people rediscover the benefits of city living,
new enclaves of the New Town are springing up to fill the
last gap sites and to take over the industrial territories of

the periphery. Whether in the longer term these areas too will come to be appreciated for their streetscape and architecture, only time will tell.

The story of each development is told in the Introduction to the appropriate Walk.

The Builders of the New Town

An army of people—architects and builders, owners and developers, craftsmen and labourers—contributed to the creation of the New Town. For those with a particular interest in architecture or the decorative arts, the history is well documented, although it can be difficult to assign the credit for a particular building or facade. A few figures, whose buildings you will encounter on several walks, stand out for their influence, innovation or sheer volume of work.

The first is **James Craig**, whose plan formed the basis of the First New Town and set out the overall approach and style. He was the son of an Edinburgh merchant and nephew to James Thomson, author of the popular poem *The Seasons,* a connection on which Craig traded heavily in his attempt to secure patronage.

Surprisingly, given his social standing, Craig was apprenticed as a mason, learning the skills of surveying and draughtsmanship. Despite winning the competition to plan the New Town at the age of only 23, Craig profited little from his creation. Although he won a few commissions including St James Square and the Royal College of Physicians in George Street, both now demolished, his career soon faltered. This may have been due to his lack of the necessary capital to take advantage of the lucrative end of architecture, the overseeing of the building process rather than the design as such. In 1782, he had to pledge his prize medal as security for a loan and he died thirteen years later, poor and largely forgotten.

While Craig failed, **Robert Adam** proved one of the most successful and influential architects of the eighteenth century. Born in Fife in 1728, the son of William Adam, an architect with an established reputation, Robert and his brother James went into the family business. As part of his training, Robert went on the Grand Tour, developing his own characteristic style from the inspiration he found in the Roman ruins of Italy and Yugoslavia. On his return, he established himself with spectacular success as a fashionable architect in London. His reputation preceded him to Edinburgh, where he designed the University, Register House and most notably Charlotte Square which sadly he did not live to see completed. It is Edinburgh's loss that his plans for St George's Church and South Bridge were not implemented.

William Playfair had perhaps an even greater impact than Adam on the appearance of the New Town. Born in London in 1789, he came to Edinburgh to live with his uncle John Playfair, Professor of Natural Philosophy at the University. No doubt the connection helped him win the competition to complete Adam's work on the University.

The success of Playfair's subsequent career was won on talent and originality. As well as major public buildings including the 'temples' at the foot of the Mound, the New

Observatory and St Stephen's Church, he planned and designed the terraces on Calton Hill as part of his largely unrealised New Town between Edinburgh and Leith. A popular figure with gentle manners, his later life was blighted by a long illness leading to his death in 1857.

Born James Gillespie in 1777, **Gillespie Graham** trained as an architectural joiner. He took the name of the heiress he married, Margaret Graham of Orchill. Now indisputably a gentleman, he relaunched his career, this time as a professional architect. He made his reputation as a designer of convincingly detailed Gothic churches, including the original St Mary's Catholic Church in Picardy Place. In this, he was assisted by his friendship with Augustus Pugin, the leading Gothic Revivalist, whom he rescued when shipwrecked and left penniless in Leith. Despite his Gothic leanings, Gillespie Graham was also capable of some of the most accomplished Classical planning, notably on the Moray Estate. It is his interpretation of the spirit of Greece and Rome which has had the greater impact on the New Town.

While many architects were involved in the design of the New Town, sculpture was virtually the province of just one man, **Sir John Steell**. Although born in Aberdeen, the son of a woodcarver, he grew up on Calton Hill. Following an apprenticeship in his father's trade, he decided to become a sculptor, spending several years in Rome to learn that exacting art. On his return, he made his reputation with his model for the large group 'Alexander and Bucephalus' now in the courtyard of the City Chambers.

Declining the advice of Francis Chantrey, the leading sculptor of the day, to move to London, he set about his mission of improving the standards of sculpture in his native land.

Steell achieved his goal, bringing about a revival in marble and large-scale bronze statuary. A successful career, including commissions from as far afield as Montreal and Calcutta, culminated in a knighthood on the unveiling of his monument to Prince Albert. He died in 1891, secure in the knowledge that his works would long outlive him. Wellington on his prancing horse outside Register House, Victoria statuesque on the pediment of the RSA, Scott sheltering from the rain under his monumental canopy, Chalmers preaching to the Princes Street shoppers: without Steell, Edinburgh would be a duller place.

Living in the New Town

While some sites, particularly in the grander streets, were taken up by rich individuals who had houses built for their own occupation, much of the New Town was developed speculatively. Builders and their backers, many of whom were Edinburgh lawyers tempted to a bit of property speculation on the side, put up houses which they then sold on, hopefully at a profit. Both landlords and developers sought to meet or anticipate market demand, each street or terrace being designed to appeal to a specific group within society, whether judges or tradesmen. Gone were the days of everyone living together in the Old Town tenements, with height from the ground rather than separation from one's neighbours determining social status.

The original developers had not appreciated the extent to which access to open space would be a selling point, but quickly responded to demand. Land was set aside in many plans for the private gardens which are such a remarkable feature of the New Town. A tenth of its total area is devoted to parkland and trees, which in maturity now screen the architecture they were intended to frame.

The houses were built in the classical style, with details taken from a well-established repertoire of pillars, pilasters and pediments inspired by ancient Greek and Rome. The facades were of finely cut limestone, generally from the Craigleith quarry to the west of the city. It is a handsome grey-white stone which hardens on exposure to the air, thus preserving finely carved detail. The quality of the stone, however, was won at a cost. The quarrymen were said to be 'Old at twenty, dead by thirty' from the lethal stone dust which coated their lungs. The much less grand backs of the houses were often built in rougher, unfinished stone to save money. Edinburgh's New Town has more than a touch of the proverbial 'fur coat and nae knickers'.

Over the years, the stonework blackened from the smoke and soot of industrial chimneys and domestic coal fires. The latter were essential to heat not only chilly drawing rooms but bedrooms, kitchens, nurseries and, if they were lucky, the servants' quarters, as the huge chimney stacks throughout the New Town bear witness. It is not surprising that Edinburgh earned its nickname of 'Auld Reekie'. With the advent of the Clean Air Acts, many New Town buildings were scrubbed to restore them to their pristine state.

This practice has now largely ceased after the discovery that cleaning damages the stone, impairing its robustness in the longer term. In the short term, the replacement of crumbling stonework can lead to some strange piebald effects.

The fine stonework of the New Town acted as the back cloth for high quality joinery; in the astragals—the wooden glazing bars in which the window panes were set—and especially in the decorative fanlights over the doors. In creating the effect of elegance without ostentation, the skills of the metalworker were also called on. Ornamental ironwork was used in balconies and the railings round the almost universal basement areas and steps. The sturdy moulded doors were given a touch of class by gleaming brasswork—name plates and finger plates, letter boxes and bell pulls. Although the overall effect was designed to be uniform, residents could express their individuality or conform to their neighbours through their choice of such details.

While the landlord laid down the overall plan, the owner or developer chose the interior layout. Almost always, this would be a variation on a standard theme. Behind an open area protected from the street by railings and bridged by the front steps, the basement would house the kitchen and other services. Extra storage could be provided in cellars under the street; increasingly the space under the stairs was pressed into use. The basement was the province of the servants, its door acting as the tradesman's entrance.

At ground level, up a short flight of steps, the main door led into a vestibule and then often a larger inner hall. Off this was the dining room, usually facing the street and behind it a parlour, bedroom, study or office if the owner conducted business from home. The inner hall led to the staircase, often lit by a glazed cupola on the roof. In the grander houses, the hall and staircase were designed to impress, with marbled columns and fancy ironwork on the banisters. The drawing room was generally on the first floor, often taking up the width of the house, its long, shuttered windows overlooking the front. Here the owner and his wife would receive visitors and entertain friends. Above were bedrooms and the nursery.

There were many variations on this theme depending on fashion, space and the dictates of the site. Where the fall of the ground permitted, there might be a second basement or even a half basement, with windows set in pits in the area pavement. Although not permitted under some of the stricter feuing conditions, dormers were often added, either at the time of building or at a later date, to make use of the attic space. The Georgian House at no 7 Charlotte Square has been carefully restored by the National Trust to something like its original condition, giving a good impression of what life must have been like in one of the New Town's grandest addresses.

Disguised behind continuous facades, many of the houses were in fact flats. A common arrangement was for a terrace of houses to be flanked by higher end blocks of flats with the main door flats having access to the basement. The palace frontages could hide some highly complex arrangements of maisonettes and penthouses! Keeping up the

Old Town tradition of living on one floor remained surprisingly popular and by no means a hardship when flats could have six bedrooms or more.

Even the New Town had its back streets, a necessity if the grander residents were to enjoy the comforts and status that having the right address in the New Town conveyed. In the original plans, shops and pubs were tucked away alongside the homes and workshops of the tradesmen and labourers, although it was not long before the fashionable shopkeepers demanded their place on Princes Street.

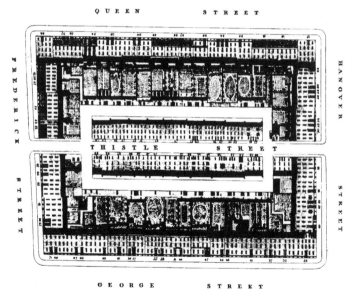

Detail from Kirkwood's New Town Plan, 1819

From the start, the New Town was designed for the relatively well off. Its appeal was greatest among the professional classes: lawyers, doctors and accountants, bankers and architects. For many years, those who could not afford to move had no choice but to remain in the Old Town, where problems of over-crowding were soon to be multiplied tenfold with the arrival of displaced and even poorer immigrants from the Highlands and Ireland.

Continuing the New Town Tradition

The professional classes remained the mainstay of the New Town. As the city grew in size and stature, commercial pressures started to intrude. Shop fronts increasingly blocked off the basement areas of the houses in the principal streets, especially in the First New Town. Houses were demolished to make way for Victorian banking halls and department stores, and Princes Street sold its soul to shopping. The simple layout of the Georgian house translated all too easily into an office.

Today, the way of life which the houses and flats were originally designed to accommodate has changed for ever. No longer can even a professional family call on the services of three or four servants or have its groceries delivered to the door. Of necessity, New Town houses have been adapted to match modern lifestyles. Even the basements and sub-basements have been brought into play as living space, their areas pressed into service as gardens, play areas, sun traps or even gymnasia. Garages and parking spaces are at a premium and there is a constant battle between the car and a town which was built for the occasional horse and carriage.

The New Town is still a thriving community. Here, people live, work, shop and entertain, very much as they have done since James Craig's plan took shape on Barebones Parks.

As you explore the grand terraces and unexpected corners of the New Town on these walks, take a discreet glance behind the astragals and the bars of the basement windows to catch a glimpse of New Town life today. Many owners take great pride in their property and have lovingly restored or re-instated the original marble fireplaces and elaborate ceiling cornices. At dusk, you may even catch sight of Leerie as he lights the lamps of Heriot Row or hear the faint clip-clop of horses' hooves in Charlotte Square.

WALK 1

NORTH

● starting and ending point of walk

Walk 1
THE FIRST NEW TOWN

North Bridge to Hanover Street

The walk starts from North Bridge, the link that made the New Town possible. After visiting two of the city's most famous pubs, you explore St Andrew Square, where the first New Town residents moved in around 1790, although some were soon displaced by Edinburgh's first financial quarter. From the oldest New Town house, the route weaves between Rose Street and George Street as far as Hanover Street before returning by Princes Street Gardens, the Scott Monument and Waverley Market. The rest of the First New Town is covered in Walk 2.

Introduction

The origins of the New Town can be traced to a pamphlet published by the Convention of Royal Boroughs in 1752 entitled *Proposals for carrying on certain Public Works in the City of Edinburgh*. The public works in question were a new Merchant's Exchange taking advantage of the site of a recently collapsed tenement in Parliament Close—now the City Chambers—and a central depository for the state records or National Registers.

The Proposals, however, went much further. They argued that the lack of appropriate accommodation forced the fashionable and the well to do to move to London or remain in the country to the detriment of both Edinburgh and Scotland. The radical solution proposed was to build a new town on modern, spacious principles along the slopes opposite the Castle ridge. This would involve draining, canalising and then bridging the swampy Nor' Loch which had for centuries acted as a natural barrier to extending the Royalty of the City.

The bridging of the Nor' Loch was not a new idea. A proposal of 1688 was overtaken by the events of the Glorious Revolution. In 1728, the Earl of Mar suggested bridges on the line eventually taken by North and South Bridge. He, in exile for his part in the 1715 Jacobite rising, was however, in no position to promote his plan.

The New Town was an idea whose time had come. Almost all of the 1752 Proposals were eventually implemented. The boldest stroke of all was the idea of extending the Union Canal to Leith, taking it right through the heart of the city. Thus, the east and west coasts of Scotland would be linked for travellers and trade. The canal boom, however, was short-lived and it was trains rather than barges that were to carve a route through Princes Street Gardens and under the Mound.

That the Proposals were realised was in large part due to their instigator, George Drummond, six times Lord Provost of Edinburgh. He had the energy and drive to push his visionary long-term plan through the self-perpetuating oli-garchy that was the Town Council.

Progress was not smooth. There were legal difficulties to be overcome and work was often halted for lack of funds. The foundation stone of North Bridge was laid with due pomp in 1763 but little happened for the next two years. In 1769, the Bridge finally opened for pedestrian traffic, only for one of its side walls to collapse killing five people. By 1772, it was fully functioning although repairs were still being paid for as late as 1784.

Meanwhile, in 1766, a competition to plan the proposed New Town was won by a 23-year-old architect, James Craig. His vision was remarkable in its simplicity and symmetry. A grid iron of three streets running along the ridge with views back to the Old Town or over the Forth Estuary to Fife would be intersected by three streets at right angles across the ridge. Each block would be fronted by grand houses with a mews lane behind for essential services. Drama would be given to the design by a square at each end with a classical church to close the vista. Craig's plan and its execution by architects of the stature of Robert Adam embodies the quest for progress and order that was at the core of the Scottish Enlightenment.

The **street names** were to be a celebration of the House of Hanover, and the united Britain on whose throne it was now firmly established. The original proposal was that the squares, named after patron saints of the United Kingdom, St Andrew and St George, would be united by George Street in honour of the King, George III. Two of the cross streets would be named Queen Street and Hanover Street after the King's spouse and his continental kingdom. The other streets were more prosaically named to commemorate their views. The remaining cross street was to be Castle Street and the streets parallel to George Street, St Giles Street and Forth Street.

When the King was shown the plans by his Scots-born physician Sir John Pringle, His Majesty took exception to St Giles Street as the name of a distinctly unsavoury area of London. Sir John tactfully suggested Prince's Street as an alternative, in honour of the Prince of Wales. He proposed replacing Forth Street by Charlotte Street after Queen Charlotte, the king's wife. The King, however, preferred Queen Street—which meant renaming the original Queen Street Frederick Street, in honour of the King's other son.

To further complicate matters, St George Square was later renamed Charlotte Square after the Queen to avoid confusion with the recently built George Square to the south of the city. The modern spelling of Princes Street, suggesting more than one royal to be honoured, only became established in the 1830s.

Although built as a residential suburb, within less than a century the First New Town had attained its present day status as the financial, business and shopping heart of a rapidly expanding city. As a result, many of the original buildings have been replaced, some more than once. Little remains of eighteenth century Princes Street although George Street and Queen Street retain something of their original character.

The City of Edinburgh Council, Lothian and Edinburgh Enterprise Ltd, Historic Scotland, Scottish Homes and the New Town Conservation Committee are to invest £30 million over the next decade in the First New Town, and the adjacent areas of the Western New Town and the Moray Estate. Over 2,000 people live in the area and over 30,000 work there. Its role is changing as many financial institutions and offices move to more modern accommodation to the south and west of the city, and as people rediscover the benefits of a city centre lifestyle. Banking halls are becoming bars and finance houses flats, and city shopping is challenged by out of town shopping centres. The aim is to tackle issues as diverse as traffic and empty property to make George Street 'the Bond Street of the North', to ensure the continuing vitality of the city centre and to reinforce the New Town's contribution to Edinburgh's reputation as a great European city.

Route

The walk starts from the corner of North Bridge and Princes Street outside the Balmoral Hotel, originally the North British or 'NB' after the railway company which owned it. On the opposite corner stands the former General Post Office, the point from which streets are numbered and distances calculated, and in a sense the very centre of Edinburgh. The building currently awaits a new use.

Start by going up **North Bridge**, the gateway to the New Town. It crosses the valley in three wide spans, sloping steadily upwards to the higher ridge of the Old Town. The first bridge was widened twice in the nineteenth century to cope with increasing volumes of traffic, before being replaced by the present structure in 1897. Bronze plates set in stone on the central spans of the bridge record its history.

Standing at the centre of the bridge, you can understand the layout of the city. To the south is the Old Town running up the ridge to the Castle while to the north, the New Town hugs the lower ridge, rising to the summit of Calton Hill with its crown of monuments. In between lies the open valley, formerly occupied by the Nor' Loch, and now by Waverley Station

The Duke of Wellington, by Steel

and Princes Street Gardens. Facing the north end of the bridge stands Robert Adam's elegant Register House (*see Walk 9*), still housing the Scottish Record Office, responsible for Scotland's registers of births, marriages and deaths. Register House is fronted by a fine equestrian statue of the Duke of Wellington by Steell.

Retrace your steps down North Bridge. Cross Princes Street at the lights, with on your left a vista along its length, the Scott Monument prominently in view. A pendulum clock, still keeping good time and advertising its maker, is set in a niche under the entrance to Register House.

Go round the left side of Register House up West Register Street, and then continue straight ahead on the paved pathway called Gabriel's Road. It once ran from the east entrance to the city to the main road north at the Stockbridge ford, cutting diagonally across the area that was to become the New Town. You will encounter it again at Gabriel's Steps (*see Walk 8*). Whether Gabriel was the Archangel or a local publican is not recorded.

Follow the lane round to the left, past two fine pubs, the first of many on this walk. Both are worth visiting. The Guildford Arms has an ornate 1890s interior with gantry, ribbed Jacobean-style ceiling and balcony bar while the Café Royal, modelled in the heyday of Scottish pub decor, boasts one of the largest island bars in Europe. The large Doulton ceramic tile panels, first displayed at the 1891 Royal Naval Exhibition, celebrate noted inventors from Caxton and his printing press to Watt and his steam engine. A bright red iron lobster advertises the Oyster Bar next door, another superb *fin de siècle* interior with stained glass sportsmen and a tiled Cunarder.

Follow West Register Street ahead to reach South St Andrew Street. On the corner across the road, the handsome red sandstone building by Alfred Waterhouse was originally the regional headquarters of the Prudential Insurance Company. The City Fathers disallowed the use of the Pru's usual corporate material, red brick. As its name suggests, Tiles, the pub on the corner that now occupies the public office, has another fine tiled interior.

Turn right into **St Andrew Square**. The first part of the New Town to be occupied, much of the Square is now lined with the opulent palaces of banking and insurance. Following the east side of the square, you pass offices of

Royal Bank of Scotland Headquarters

the Royal Bank and the Bank of Scotland, rivalling one another in their appearance of confident prosperity.

Next door, set back behind a formal carriageway, is the headquarters of the Royal Bank of Scotland. It occupies the house built in 1771 for Sir Laurence Dundas, the son of an Edinburgh Baillie, who made his fortune as commissary-general responsible for supplying the British army in Flanders in the 1750s. His house usurped the site intended by James Craig for the church of St Andrew, to balance that of St George in Charlotte Square at the opposite end of George Street. The Bank bought the house in 1820.

The banking hall inside with its starry dome is worth a visit if the Bank is open. Outside stands an equestrian statue of one of the Bank's most eminent directors, John Hope, the fourth Earl of Hopetoun, who took over command of the British army at Corunna after the death of Sir John Moore. The inscription is repeated in Latin on the reverse of the plinth.

> Stately as it looks today, **St Andrew Square** was once the scene of a horrific murder. In 1717, Robert Irvine, licensed to preach by the Church of Scotland and tutor to the children of a gentleman who lived in nearby Broughton, took advantage of a maidservant while the children's parents were out. One of the children gave the game away. Although the parents decided to overlook Irvine's indiscretion, the experience caused him to lose his reason.
>
> On the pretext of taking the two boys on a country stroll, he lured them to the field on which St Andrew Square now stands and beheaded them with a knife. Spotted by some passers-by, he tried to turn the knife on himself and then to drown himself in the Water of Leith. As a final twist to his fate, before execution his hands were chopped off by the murder weapon.

Immediately after the Royal Bank headquarters, you pass one of the earliest houses to be built in the New Town, dating from 1769, and then the contribution of two centuries later, Edinburgh's utilitarian main bus station. No gesture to the romance of travel here!

Cross the road at the lights. As you head down North St Andrew Street, the view opens out over the New Town across the Forth Estuary to Fife. Turn left into Queen Street past the red sandstone Gothic Scottish National Portrait Gallery. Designed by Sir Rowand Anderson in 1885, this Venetian palace was financed by J R Findlay, the proprietor of the *Scotsman* newspaper. Figures of characters from

Scottish history decorate the facade and the painted frieze in the main hall. The Portrait Gallery commemorates the Scottish great and the good of all periods, including many distinguished New Town residents.

At the end of the Gallery turn left into Findlay Court, a little courtyard with seats and a pebble picture of a thistle with an owl, a dipper, a squirrel and a lizard.

Turn right down the lane behind to reach North Saint David Street. On the near side, the houses are early while across the road are some of Edinburgh's bleakest 1960s and 70s office blocks.

Cross by the lights and turn left and then right into Thistle Street. A little way along on the left is Thistle Court, containing the first houses to be built in the New Town. Facing each other across a garden, these modest dwellings are now quite out of character with their starkly functional surroundings.

Return to North St David Street and turn right. Across the road, the north side of St Andrew Square still retains some of its original houses. The gable at the end of the row has dummy windows, a typically Georgian feature originally introduced as a means of avoiding the Window Tax while maintaining the balance of the facades.

Henry Dundas, first Viscount Melville, looks down from his pillar in the centre of the Square. During the late eighteenth century, he controlled most of the government patronage in Scotland earning him the title of 'Henry the Ninth, the uncrowned king of Scotland'.

Continue along the west side of the Square to cross **George**

Street. Ahead stands the Scott Monument with a glimpse of the crown of St Giles behind. The view along George Street extends all the way to Charlotte Square and the cupola of the former St George's Church beyond the trees.

Carry straight on into South St David Street past the handsome black and white 1930s office built for the Guardian Royal Exchange Assurance, with its carved wooden doors. Note the stone inscription on no 21 commemorating the residence of David Hume, philosopher, historian and famous atheist. He was one of many who moved into the fashionable New Town after living most of his life in the closes of the Old Town. He rebutted the contemporary joke that the street was named after him by commenting wryly that many worse men had been canonised!

Turn right into **Rose Street**, past the back of Jenners, the world's oldest independent department store and a long-standing Edinburgh institution. Its iron and glass hall rising the full height of the building is worth a visit and its tearoom allows you to eavesdrop on genteel Edinburgh.

Shopping in Edinburgh might have been very different if, in 1837, Charles **Jenner** and his friend Charles Kennington had not decided to go to the races despite having been refused the time off. As a result, they lost their jobs and decided to set up 'Kennington and Jenner' on the corner of Princes Street and South St David Street. Through their hard work, the corner shop flourished. In 1892, disaster struck as a huge inferno engulfed the building. Nothing daunted, Charles Jenner started again from scratch. A man of academic leanings, he instructed that the design should be modelled, not on Liberty's or Harrods but on the

Bodleian Library in Oxford, requesting that caryatids should be carved into the columns as 'women are the support of our house.' Their calm gaze still follows the throngs of Princes Street shoppers a century later.

Pass the Abbotsford on the corner of the lane, another magnificent Edwardian interior with an ornate gantry and island bar. After the Dome Garden Cafe with palms and tree ferns in pots, take the lane on the right through two gates back to George Street. A handsome Corinthian portico fronts the Dome, another banking hall now given over to liquid currency. Designed by David Rhind in 1857, the building was formerly the headquarters of the Commercial Bank of Scotland. The magnificent domed banking hall which its name celebrates is worth a visit.

Another Corinthian portico, this time topped by a spire, fronts the opposite side of the street. This is the oval Church of St Andrew and St George, displaced from Craig's intended position by Sir Laurence Dundas's house in St Andrew Square. Mr Young, who owned the George Street site, insisted that as a condition of his moving to an adjacent plot, there should be 'no burying' in or round the church. Young's new house is now buried behind the facade of the adjoining George Hotel.

The **George Hotel** has grown steadily since it started life as three houses in the 1780s. A century later, the ground floor was converted into offices for the Caledonian Insurance Company while the upper floors became a hotel. The main dining room of the George retains the grand dome and marbled pillars of Scotland's first banking hall.

In the late 1950s, plans for a 17-storey extension at the back of the hotel were stopped by a public inquiry.

Turn left to reach **Hanover Street**, passing on the left the Royal Society of Edinburgh, Scotland's leading scientific and learned society, founded in 1783 under a Royal

Statue of George IV

Charter for the 'Advancement of Learning and Useful Knowledge'. In the middle of the intersection stands the statue of George IV commemorating his visit to the city in 1822, the first by a reigning monarch for nearly two hundred years.

Turn left down Hanover Street. In the basement on the left, at the corner of Rose Street, is Edinburgh's most famous literary pub, Milne's Bar.

In the 1950s and 1960s, **Milne's Bar** was the haunt of poets, writers, left-wingers and swingers, presided over by the triumvirate of Hugh MacDiarmid, Norman MacCaig and Sydney Goodsir Smith. Visitors included Stevie Smith, Dylan Thomas and W H Auden. Evenings in Milne's did much to revive writing in the Scots language. A board by the door relates the history of the pub and inside there are framed photos and poems of some of the luminaries.

Opposite are two more palaces to commerce, the Merchant's Hall, built as the ill-fated City of Glasgow Bank in

1865, and the even more grandiosely pillared TSB, dating from 1939. At the foot of the street stands the pillared facade of Playfair's Royal Scottish Academy surmounted by Steell's large figure of Queen Victoria.

Cross **Princes Street** at the traffic lights to reach the paved area at the foot of **the Mound**, a popular stance for pipers, and during the Festival, one of the main venues for street theatre. Behind it is another Playfair temple housing the National Gallery of Scotland.

Turn left into **Princes Street Gardens** just behind the modern shelter in the guise of a temple. On your right, you can spot the windows of the ingeniously inserted basement extension to the National Gallery. There are plans to use a similar disguise in creating a new shopping gallery under Princes Street itself.

As you stroll along, note the inscriptions on the benches, a peculiarly Edinburgh tradition. Those remembered by the donors range from local worthies and institutions to visitors from around the world who fell in love with the city. Some of the inscriptions are quite moving. Even John Lennon has his bench close to the Scott Monument, courtesy of the Edinburgh Beatles Appreciation Society.

On your left, Princes Street retains nothing of its original uniformity. It is a real hotchpotch of levels, styles and architectural quality. Some of the more modern shops retain first floor balconies, the relic of an abandoned 1960s plan to develop a walkway with access to shops on two levels, on the model of medieval Chester.

Across the Gardens rises the slope of the Old Town,

with the baroque headquarters of the Bank of Scotland in the vanguard.

> The **Scott Monument**, a Gothic rocket under which impassively sit Sir Walter and his favourite deerhound, Maida, is the New Town's most distinctive, if incongruous, memorial. Although you can normally ascend it by a tortuous stair for fine views over the New Town, it is currently closed for repairs to its crumbling statuary.
>
> Funded by a subscription raised on Scott's death in 1832, the Monument was designed by George Meikle Kemp, a carpenter and self-taught architect. He actually came third in the design competition but after much argument and requests for further drawings, the Committee awarded him the job. Tragically he did not live to see his design completed, accidentally drowning in the Union Canal basin after losing his way one dark night.

Just beyond the Scott Monument there is a statue to David Livingstone, the Scots-born medical missionary and explorer, who opened up a large area of central Africa to trade and Empire while by his own admission converting only one native soul.

Cross **Waverley Bridge**, with its pipers, tour buses and station entrance, and head for the granite paved top of Waverley Market a few yards along Princes Street on your right. Formerly a market, and then an exhibition venue, it is now a speciality shopping mall. Follow the paved way along the side of the mall, with views through the windows at an unusual angle.

Go along the terrace parallel to Waverley Station with fine views of the Old Town and North Bridge to the courtyard of the **Tourist Information Centre**, which has books and other souvenirs for sale and a ticket and accommodation booking service.

Return to Princes Street past the flags of many nations and three bronzed figures which are not tourists. Turn right along Princes Street past the head of Waverley Steps, which lead down to the station. This is reputedly the windiest spot in Edinburgh. The liveried footmen waiting inside the grand entrance to the Balmoral Hotel mean that your are close to the corner of North Bridge and the start of the walk.

Walk 2
MOVING WEST

Hanover Street to the West End

From the foot of the Mound, the walk threads its way through the streets, grand and simple, of the First New Town as it moved west in line with Craig's original plan. The climax is Robert Adam's Charlotte Square, the New Town's grandest composition. A visit to St John's and St Cuthbert's Churches and their graveyards is followed by a stroll back through Princes Street Gardens.

Introduction
The First New Town developed steadily from east to west. Hanover Street was started in 1784, Frederick Street in 1786 and Castle Street in 1792. In 1785, the Town Council purchased the land which they did not already own west of Castle Street. There remained one problem. Land belonging to the Earl of Moray cut across the north west corner of Craig's proposed west square. The Council contemplated substituting a smaller circus for the square but fortunately, a settlement was eventually reached.

The valley between the Old and New Towns, formerly

WALK 2

NORTH

● starting and ending point of walk

the Nor' Loch, remained an unattractive piece of swampy waste ground. Nonetheless, the owners of the houses in Princes Street valued their open outlook and views of the Castle. When, in 1776, some low buildings to the west of North Bridge threatened to set a precedent, the proprietors took court action. They argued that they had bought their feus on the basis of Craig's plan, which showed no building on the south side of Princes Street. Although they won their case, a supplementary ruling held that west of Hanover Street, the Council had the right to feu provided that any new building was kept more than 96 feet away from the Princes Street properties.

This set the scene for future battles, tentative moves by the Council being vigorously resisted by the Proprietors. Matters came to a head in 1816 when the Council obtained an Act of Parliament permitting the erection of a church, St John's, on the site of a market garden at the West End. The proprietors succeeded in inserting a provision in the Act outlawing any further building on the south side west of the Mound, except for a gardener's lodge and greenhouses.

The Act also authorised the proprietors to lease the Gardens from the Council and to raise money to drain and improve them. Alexander Douglas WS, known as 'Dirty Douglas' because of his slovenly appearance, was appointed Treasurer. Despite his nickname, he conducted affairs efficiently. On his death in 1851 Douglas was succeeded by his son who held the post until the Gardens were handed over to the public in 1876.

By 1821 the swampy ground was drained and leases

negotiated for the adjoining land belonging to the Castle and the owner of Ramsay Garden. Access to the Gardens was initially restricted to owners of houses in Princes Street, but from 1821 keys were sold to others for a subscription of four guineas a year. Sir Walter Scott was granted an honorary key in 1827.

Other threats to the tranquillity of the Gardens were less easily resisted. An attempt to drive a railway through the Gardens was successfully fought off in Parliament in 1836. By 1844, however, the proprietors decided that 'the inroad could not be prevented altogether'. They settled for £1,000 in compensation and an agreement that the line should be concealed in a cutting at the railway company's expense.

As the nineteenth century progressed, housing increasingly gave way to shops. Pressure was growing for the public to have access to the Gardens and reluctant concessions were made. By 1851, the cost of a key had fallen to one guinea. Two years later, the Governor of the Castle made admission of the public a condition of continuing the popular military band concerts in the Gardens. He suggested that the advertisements for the concerts should clearly state that the 'lower orders' would not be admitted, and that nursemaids with children would be banned, as children disturbed the music. The proprietors conceded that 'persons of respectability' should be allowed in.

The Town Council offered not only to waive the rent but to make a payment if the Gardens were open to the public two or three days a week. After taking legal advice the Proprietors concluded, with at least affected regret, that they could not agree, on the grounds that they could be subject to challenge by any individual proprietor who thought his rights had been infringed.

There matters rested until 1875 when the Council, taking the bull by the horns, announced that they were going to apply for an Act of Parliament to take the Gardens into public ownership. The proprietors, many by now shop-owners rather than residents, decided not to contest the bill, on condition that up to £5,000 was spent on widening and improving Princes Street to cope with the horse-drawn trams. The Gardens thus remain today part of the unique landscape of the city and open to the enjoyment of all.

Route

The walk starts from the foot of the Mound, in front of the Royal Scottish Academy.

As its name suggests, **the Mound** was where builders were allowed to dump the earth dug from the foundations of the New Town. An informal route grew up across the pile of earth, known as 'Geordie Boyd's mud brig' after a clothier who took early steps to improve it. The Town Council officially adopted it as a route in 1781. Later the Mound was also used as a pitch for circuses and other entertainments including a circular Panorama, the precursor of the wide screen cinema. 'Paris at Night' must have pulled in the crowds.

The first permanent building on the Mound was the

The Royal Scottish Academy

Royal Institution, now the Royal Scottish Academy, an art gallery in the form of a Doric Greek temple. It was designed by William Playfair in 1822 and extended less than a decade later. In 1853 Playfair was commissioned to provide a second temple, Ionic this time, to house the National Gallery of Scotland.

The difficulty of extending the colonnaded National Gallery was ingeniously overcome in 1975 by adding a gallery underneath, its windows opening off East Princes Street Gardens. The Gallery houses a collection of Old Masters, including works by El Greco, Rembrandt, Vermeer and Poussin as well as the national collection of Scottish painting, while the neighbouring Royal Scottish Academy holds temporary exhibitions.

Walk up the Mound along the side of the Royal Scottish Academy and turn left between the two galleries. Turning left again towards Princes Street you will find a bronze relief model of the city with lettering in Braille. It gives a good impression of the layout of the Old and New Towns on their parallel ridges. Set in the paving nearby is the UNESCO World Heritage Site symbol conferred on the Old and New Towns in 1995. The paved area around the galleries is often lively with street performers, arts and craft stalls and kilted pipers of variable quality.

Return to Princes Street and cross at the lights. Turn left to cross Hanover Street and then turn right up its west side. Turn left along George Street to pass the arcaded Assembly Rooms. A venue for balls, promenades and concerts, they were completed in 1787, replacing similar accommodation in New Assembly Close off the High Street. The move meant that the New Town had 'made it' in the eyes of high society. The Assembly Rooms are still a centre of the city's cultural life, hosting a wide range of functions and Festival events.

Just beyond is the Standing Order, another grand banking hall with granite pillars supporting a top-lit dome, which has been transformed into a pub. The building was formerly the Edinburgh head office of Glasgow's Union Bank. William Pitt the Younger, Prime Minister during the Napoleonic Wars, directs the traffic at the intersection with Frederick Street. The statue by Francis Chantrey was erected in 1833 by the Tory faithful. Believing that they were unlikely ever to return to Government, given the increase in

47

the electorate brought about by the Reform Act, they considered their cause best served by commemorating past days of glory.

Cross Frederick Street and turn left and then right into the Rose Street pedestrian precinct.

> Artisans and tradesmen serving the more affluent households were the first residents of **Rose Street** and neighbouring Thistle Street. Some of the original modest houses remain, although nearly all now function as shops.
>
> By the mid-nineteenth century, Rose Street had assumed a more raffish character, both sides of the street being lined with pubs. Although much of the New Town was 'dry', hostelries were discreetly housed at the corners of mews and lanes, out of sight and earshot of polite society. With its tiles, stained glass, elaborate woodwork and mirrors, the Kenilworth is a magnificent survival of a late Victorian pub interior. More recently, Rose Street has acquired a reputation as *the* place for a pub crawl after Rugby internationals.

On reaching **Castle Street** turn right. Opposite, No 32 was the birthplace of Kenneth Grahame, Secretary of the Bank of England from 1898-1908, now much better known as the author of *The Wind in the Willows*. As you reach George Street, the administrative headquarters of the Church of Scotland, known throughout the Ministry as 121, loom large on your left on the opposite side of the street.

Cross George Street at the zebra crossings. Long out of fashion, these were recently reinstated to give a higher priority to pedestrians. The statue at this intersection is of Thomas Chalmers, Professor of Divinity at Edinburgh University, philanthropist and leader of the Disruption in 1843, when 472 ministers of the Church of Scotland walked out en masse in protest at lay patronage (*see Walk 8*).

Look back along George Street towards St Andrew Square. Towards the far end of the block opposite can just be seen the flashing light of the lighthouse outside the headquarters of the Northern Lighthouse Board. The Board is responsible for looking after Scotland's lighthouses, although no longer their keepers, the last of whom was replaced by an automatic light in 1998.

Turn right down Castle Street, a street of character which

No 39 Castle Street

retains many of its original houses. No 39, which forms part of an impressive pillared and pedimented facade with atypical bow windows, was for many years the home of Sir Walter Scott. The block is a good example of the way that different sizes of houses were fitted in behind a single facade. 39-43 was constructed as two two-storey dwellings with basements and a penthouse flat running the length of the building.

Cross Castle Street to enter **Young Street**, a pleasant cobbled lane with many of the original houses built for 'the better class of artisan'. At one end is the Oxford Bar, the haunt of crime fiction's Inspector Rebus, and at the other its rival, the Cambridge. A barber's shop sports the traditional striped pole. An unfortunate effect of recent traffic management experiments has been to make Young Street something of a rat-run.

At the end of Young Street, turn right into North Charlotte Street. At the foot, the Drum and Monkey claims to be one of the world's top five hundred bars. Look across to St Colme Street on the left and Albyn Place to the right, marking the start of the Moray Estate (*see Walk 5*). While Albyn Place's facade aspires to grandeur, St Colme Street is more modest, careful not to intrude on the views from the houses of Charlotte Square. Archibald Campbell-Swinton, pioneer of the modern electronic system of television, was born at no 9 Albyn Place.

Cross North Charlotte Street at the lights, passing the large Gothic monument to Catherine Sinclair. Her philanthropy was wide ranging, from soup kitchens and public drinking fountains to running schools where poor girls were trained for domestic service. She was also the author of popular children's books.

Turn left back up the hill and right, along the north side of Charlotte Square.

Spurred on by criticism of the quality of some of their New Town buildings, the Town Council commissioned Robert Adam, the most famous architect of his day and an Edinburgh man, to produce a plan to be imposed on anyone wishing to build in **Charlotte Square.** Adam's brief was to design facades, 'not much ornamented but of an elegant simplicity'. He delivered a masterpiece. The facades give the impression of palaces rather than rows of town houses. They provided the model on which much of the subsequent development of the New Town was based.

Until recently, Charlotte Square was the centre of Edinburgh's financial services community and able to command the highest rentals. Although many firms have since moved to Edinburgh's new financial centre round Lothian Road, Charlotte Square remains, as it always was, a very prestigious address.

On the north side you pass the official residence of the Secretary of State for Scotland at Bute House (no 6), and of the Moderator of the Church of Scotland, who has a flat on the upper storeys of no 7, the Georgian House. Open to the public under the auspices of the National Trust for Scotland, the Georgian House gives a feel for what life was like in a New Town household in its hey-day. Note the high pavements with mounting blocks to assist the gentry into their carriages and the snuffers on the railings for extinguishing the torches that guided them on dark nights before the elegant gaslights were fitted.

At the next corner, see if you can spot the pretenders. Although the style of the houses running down the hill opposite is Georgian, they are not what they seem. Their spick and span stonework gives a clue to their date of building—1989! This was one of the last green field sites in the New Town to be filled.

Cross Glenfinlas Street and continue along the west side of the Square. Sir William Fettes, merchant, twice Lord Provost and founder of the leading Edinburgh public school, lived at no 13, while no 14 was the home of Lord Cockburn.

A Law Lord and author, **Lord Cockburn** was also an early conservationist. He was very much in two minds about the New Town, fondly reminiscing about the summer evenings when he could listen to 'the ceaseless rural corncraiks nestling happily in the dewy grass' further down the hill.

He played a leading part in the campaigns to prevent building on the south side of Princes Street and tried in vain to stop the railway steaming through the Gardens. Cockburn's *Memorials of His Time* give a wonderful picture of life in Edinburgh as it made the transition from Old Town to New Town. His name has been adopted by the Cockburn Association, Edinburgh's leading conservation society.

In the middle of the west side of the Square, as Craig's plan required, stands St George's Church, by Robert Reid. Unfortunately, Adam's design was rejected, probably on grounds of cost. With the decline in the resident New Town population, the congregation of St George's was merged with that of St Andrew's in George Street, and in 1964 the church became West Register House, an outstation of the Scottish Record Office.

In the centre of Charlotte Square, looking rather forlorn, stands Edinburgh's memorial to Victoria's Prince Albert, mounted and in a Field Marshall's uniform. The statue was commissioned from the ubiquitous John Steell who was knighted for his trouble. In spring, the private gardens are bright with crocuses and daffodils and during the annual Book Festival, with tents and authors. For the rest of the year, Albert has them to himself.

Cross over to the south side of the Square. No 24 was the birthplace of a real Field Marshall, Earl Haig of First World War fame, or notoriety, depending on your point of view. Its basement is now a wine bar. Numbers 26 and 27 are currently in poor repair, with some of the brasswork removed, a symptom of the decline in the fortunes of the Square. The National Trust for Scotland has recently purchased six houses to form a new headquarters and exhibition gallery. Restoration to their former glory is in hand.

Turn right into South Charlotte Street. A plaque on the first house on the right marks the birthplace and childhood home of Alexander Graham Bell, the inventor of the telephone. His father taught elocution and speech to the deaf before the family emigrated to Canada to escape the ravages of tuberculosis, to which two of Bell's brothers had already succumbed. BT plans to open the house to the public as a lasting celebration of Bell's achievement and the telecommunications revolution which he pioneered.

Cross Princes Street and turn right along the side of the graceful Perpendicular Church of St John the Evangelist, built to a design by William Burn in 1816. The stone crown on top of the tower blew down in a gale before the Church was even finished, a detail not to be repeated.

Turn left into **Lothian Road**. Being Episcopalian, the

Church's open doors beckon visitors throughout the week. Inside, tall, slender pillars support the fans and pendants of a roof modelled on Henry VII's chapel in Westminster Abbey and lit by what is claimed to be the best collection of stained glass in Scotland. Curiosities include the library of the longest-lived suffragette and the monument to a soldier who took part in Custer's Last Stand.

Turn left down a short flight of stairs past the Church's cafe and international craft shop. Tucked away against the east end of the church is a small graveyard. Here lies Henry Raeburn, Scotland's greatest portrait painter (*see Walk 7*), and Margaret Rutherford, the mother of Sir Walter Scott. In death, Scott's father remained true to the Old Town, being buried in Greyfriars Churchyard.

Head up the ramp to Princes Street and turn right past a large Celtic Cross commemorating Dean Ramsay. Take the flight of steps down to St Cuthbert's Church. A parallel path goes down to a useful, if hard to find, two-storey public convenience.

Taking its name from a church at the foot of the Castle Rock, founded supposedly by the Northumbrian saint, **St Cuthbert's** was once the parish church for the whole area now covered by the New Town. The present Renaissance-style building dates only from 1892, although the spire is a century older. The rather clumsy lines of the church have led to its description as the box from which the dainty St John's has been unpacked.

The churchyard is worth exploring, a record in stone of New Town life. On the side of the Church facing you is a seventeenth-century coat of arms with a vault beneath. A survival from an earlier building, this is the 'lair' of Nisbet of Dean, the owner of the land across Dean Bridge (*see Walk 6*). A notoriously mean man, his non-payment of his workers resulted in a strike, which the Kirk Session were forced to settle in order to get the area tidied up. It took seven years and an action in the Sheriff Court to recoup the costs from Nisbet. Yet the inscription claims he preferred 'Fame to Riches and Virtue to Fame'! On the west wall, a nineteenth-century minister, Dr David Dickson, blesses children in perpetuity, while the sundial and tower clock above record the inexorable passage of time.

Take the flight of steps to your left. The path bends right past a row of lairs and then left round the back of them. Here you will find the toppled-over tomb of Thomas de Quincey, author of *Confessions of an Opium Eater*—perhaps vandalised by an opponent of the drug culture. Next to him is a touching wall memorial to Rufus Woodward, a Yale graduate who came to the city to continue his studies and, apparently unsuccessfully, to restore his health. His Edinburgh friends knew him as 'the amiable American stranger'.

Keep on the path which bends back on itself to reach the circular watchtower near the Lothian Road gate. At one time well outside the city, the isolated churchyard was an obvious target for 'Resurrection Men' or grave-robbers in the business of stealing bodies to sell to Edinburgh's flourishing anatomy schools. The watchtower and high churchyard walls were an attempt to foil them.

Return by the broad path along the south side of the church to the gold painted gate into Princes Street Gardens. Ahead, past the playground and cafe is a florid, rusty gold fountain.

> Of French manufacture, the enormous cast iron **Ross Fountain** was purchased from the International Exhibition of 1862 and donated to the city by a wealthy gunsmith, Daniel Ross. Its reception was not entirely favourable. Dean Ramsay, the incumbent of St John's for over 40 years, described the figures on the top as 'Grossly indecent and disgusting: insulting and offensive to the moral feelings of the community'. At the top of the slope Dr Thomas Guthrie, the founder of Ragged Schools for the children of the nineteenth century Old Town slums, firmly turns his broad back to it.

Take the path between rows of commemorative benches towards the Ross Bandstand, a summer entertainment venue for everything from jazz to children's talent contests. The large granite boulder to the right of the path commemorates the Norwegian Brigade raised in Scotland after the fall of Norway to Hitler.

Turn left up to the terrace below Princes Street and continue eastwards. A dashing mounted soldier tops a Boer War Memorial to the Scots Greys, while on the right an interpretation board explains the geological history of the Castle rock and Old Town ridge. The covered seating faces south to catch the sun while the keeper's cottage lends a touch of domesticity to the formal lawns and flowerbeds.

Climb the steps at the end to reach Edinburgh's famous

Statue of Allan Ramsay

floral clock. The face and even the hands are planted every summer with brightly coloured flowers—and a cuckoo performs on the hour! Beside the clock is a statue to Allan Ramsay, the poet and father of the painter of the same name, whose works can be seen in the National Gallery of Scotland ahead. Ramsay ranks second only to Raeburn among Scottish portrait painters. The family owned the house, nick-named Goose Pie House because of its shape, which now forms the centrepiece of Ramsay Garden, the romantic gabled and turreted extravagance to the left of the Castle.

Cross the Mound to reach the start of the walk.

WALK 3

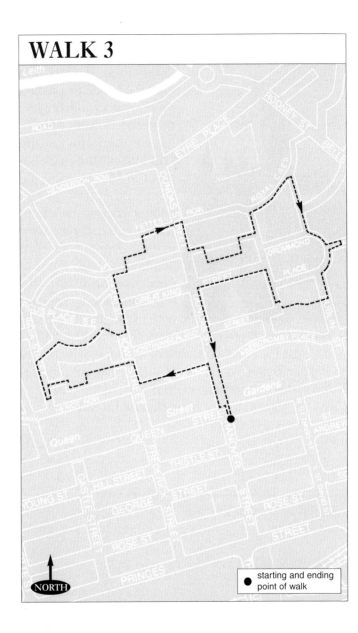

NORTH

● starting and ending
point of walk

Walk 3
THE SECOND NEW TOWN

Queen Street to Fettes Row

This walk explores the Second New Town paralleling the first New Town to the north. Prestigious Heriot Row is followed by its working class neighbour, Jamaica Street, and then by the sloping circle of Royal Circus. The walk follows the abrupt lower edge of the New Town along Fettes Row to Royal Crescent before turning up to the grand finale of Drummond Place and Great King Street.

Introduction

As the end of the eighteenth century approached, the First New Town was nearing completion. After a slow start, the Town Council's scheme had proved a great success. It was time for the private developers to move in.

North of Queen Street Gardens, most of the land belonged to the Heriot's Trust. The Trust had originally been set up under the will of 'Jinglin' Geordie' Heriot, goldsmith, millionaire and moneylender to James VI, to endow a Hospital or charity school in Lauriston Place. The Trust, a major landowner in the city by the end of the eighteenth century, had feued thirteen acres to a lawyer, David Stewart. It was Stewart who took the initiative in developing the Second New Town. He approached the trustees with a plan for a joint development based on a major street running east-west parallel to Queen Street, ending in a square to the east and a circus to the west. At the foot of the hill a crescent was envisaged with open views towards the Forth.

Although Stewart went bankrupt in 1800 before development could start, the plan finally adopted was essentially his. The square and circus were reduced in size and smaller roads were added, north and south of the main axis. Building began in 1803, starting at the top of the hill and working down, in accordance with the final plans drawn up by William Sibbald and Robert Reid. The end of the Napoleonic Wars provided a spur to the development, which was largely complete by 1823.

Unlike much of the First New Town, the trustees laid down strict conditions for the height and overall layout of the houses, aiming to ensure uniformity of appearance while allowing some variation in decoration and detailed design. Little altered over the years and the area still gives a good impression of the effect the planners sought to achieve: elegance without ostentation.

Route

The walk begins at the intersection of Queen Street and Hanover Street. To reach this point from Princes Street, start at the Mound, walk up the right hand side of Hanover Street, cross George Street and continue on Hanover Street down the hill.

Cross **Queen Street**, the northern boundary of the First New Town, and look back along its length. Despite some later frontages, it still gives an impression of what Princes Street must have looked like when first built. How did the proprietors of Queen Street feel as they watched the upstart Second New Town rising at their feet? Opposite, a few doors along on your left, is one of Queen Street's grandest houses, built by Robert Adam for the Baron Orde in 1770 and now part of the Royal College of Physicians.

Continue down the hill alongside Queen Street Gardens. What appears to be a folly, in the form of a small Greek temple in the middle of the Gardens, is in fact a cleverly disguised gas regulation station. Like most New Town Gardens, Queen Street is private, keys being issued only to the owners of the adjoining houses and offices who pay a subscription for their upkeep.

On reaching the next corner, look down the slope of the Second New Town. The distant view changes constantly with the weather. If the Fife hills look little more than a stone's throw away, rain is in the air. To the right lies Abercromby Place, its curve no more than an expedient to avoid a piece of land which its Queen Street proprietor refused to sell. Perhaps for this reason, it lacks conviction.

Cross Abercromby Place and Dundas Street, the northern extension of Hanover Street, and turn left into **Heriot Row**. With its garden outlook, parking and relative peace, it is one of the New Town's most sought-after addresses.

Heriot Row

Each block has a higher elevation at both ends and a pediment in the middle but Reid's design lacks the drama of Adam's Charlotte Square.

Towards the far end of the first block, no 17 was the childhood home of Robert Louis Stevenson. The inscription on the plaque is a verse from his poem to 'Leerie', the lamplighter who would go round at dusk lighting the gas lamps outside each house. Often confined to bed through illness as a child, Stevenson would await his Leerie's arrival with longing. *Treasure Island* may have been inspired by an island in the pond in the gardens opposite.

Cross Howe Street and turn right down the hill. The end of the street is closed by the massive tower frontage of St Stephen's Church. Turn left into Jamaica Street, the only street in the Second New Town originally planned as working class housing. The two rows of simple tenements were demolished in 1960 to make way for the improved amenities of the present courtyard flats.

Go straight ahead through the entrance arch to Jamaica Mews and across the courtyards, a sun trap for neighbourhood cats. At the far end is Kay's Bar which retains much of the fittings and atmosphere of Kay's wine shop which opened here in 1815.

Cross **India Street** which retains much of its original roadway with its setts, cobbled gutters and stone kerb crossings. Go a few steps up the hill to reach no 14, once the home of James Clerk Maxwell.

> Although an unsung hero in the city of his childhood, the physicist **James Clerk Maxwell** (1831-1879) ranks alongside Newton and Einstein. Brought up in Galloway, the son of a wealthy family, he came to the capital to attend Edinburgh Academy, where his country accent and eccentric ways earned him the nickname 'Dafty'. A brilliant if bullied teenager, his first scientific paper was read to the luminaries of the Royal Society of Edinburgh when he had just turned fifteen.
>
> Later Professor at Aberdeen, then Cambridge University—Edinburgh turned him down—he produced the first colour photograph and laid the foundations for the science of statistical mechanics. His most notable achievement was Maxwell's equations, showing that light was an electromagnetic wave, and predicting the existence of radio waves and other electromagnetic radiations. He can justly be regarded as the 'father of electronics'. The house now belongs to the James Clerk Maxwell Foundation and houses the International Centre for Mathematical Sciences.

Retrace your steps down the hill. Wide basement areas reflect the lifestyles of the New Town—aspiring and established, alternative and fashionable, green and green-fingered.

Re-cross India Street, turn right into Circus Gardens and then right again to go round **Royal Circus**. Set on a slope and bisected by the busy North West Circus Place, Royal

Circus is a grand set piece that has not quite managed to pull it off. The gardens with their mature trees divide it further, creating the impression of two quietly elegant crescents. Only the curious street numbering, odd numbers in one half and even in the other, attempts to draw the Circus together.

As you turn into Royal Circus, look over to the other half for a view of no 24, the home of Sir Henry Littlejohn, Edinburgh's first Medical Officer of Health. His damning report on the poverty and ill-health of the Old Town slums drew the Council's attention back from the glories of the New Town to the squalor on its own doorstep.

Turn right again into South East Circus Place, to rejoin Howe Street. Cross it and turn left to cross Great King Street. A vista extends to Drummond Place, the balancing square to the east. At the foot of Howe Street stands St Stephen's Church. It was originally to be the showpiece of Royal Circus, signing off the west end of Great King Street. A change of plan, however, led the Council to purchase this more difficult, sloping site instead. Set the challenge of designing

Royal Circus

a Church to fit this awkward space, William Playfair came up with his unusual design, essentially a square set diagonally so that the tower abuts a corner.

Because of the steeply falling site, the main entrance once led into the gallery of the church, now separately floored, with the 'body of the kirk' below. The clock in the tower claims to have the longest pendulum in Europe at 65 feet, 9 inches! St Stephen's dwarfs its neighbour, the small Gothic St Vincent's, still functioning as a Church unlike the former, which as the Stockbridge Centre seeks a new role as an arts or community resource.

Turn right into **Cumberland Street**. The first house on the left carries the distinctive plaque of the Edinburgh New Town Conservation Committee, a white leaf in the shape of an anthemion—a leitmotif of Greek architecture—on a terracotta ground. You will find a number of these plaques, especially in this part of the New Town, where by the 1960s many of the flats and houses were in a poor state of repair. Each plaque gives the original date of the building and when it was restored. The New Town is the Forth Bridge in stone, in need of continuous repair.

Take the lane to the left, by the side of a car park. Some of the houses in Cumberland Street even have their own garages underneath! At the end of the car park, take the narrow cobbled lane to the left, climbing the steps to reach **Fettes Row**.

With Fettes Row, the New Town comes to an abrupt end. Beyond lay the industrial suburb of Silvermills. In 1812, the residents of Great King Street were up in arms when Mr

Lauder, a skinner by trade, opened a new tannery with a steam engine. The valley is still 'industrial' though the noxious fumes are long gone and the industry is insurance.

Cross to the north side of Fettes Row to appreciate the effect of a half-built terrace. Numbers 23/24, subject of the first New Town conservation project, were designed to be the centrepiece rather than the end block of Fettes Row with a second terrace of equal length to the west. The Council's choice of site for St Stephen's Church meant that the plans had to be altered. The shape of the available land dictated that the new terrace would have to be convex. It was never built. The setback of discovering an old quarry used for building part of the Old Town was compounded by a shortage of funds. By 1840, investor interest had switched to the railways.

Turn right along Fettes Row and cross Dundas Street. Turn right and first left into Cumberland Street, lined with plain, three-storey tenements for artisans and tradesmen. Turn right into South East Cumberland Street Lane, a fine mews with the large gardens and coach houses of Great King Street on the right and the small sloping gardens of the houses in Cumberland Street on the left. Here, the hierarchical, social planning of the New Town is very clear. The higher up the hill and the more open the outlook, the higher one's social status.

Turn right again at the end of the mews, to reach Dundonald Street where you turn left. Stepping down the steep hill, notice that the houses have deep basement areas, the windows of sub-basements being set in cylindrical pits in the paving.

Turn right along **Royal Crescent**. Started in the 1820s, its Greek classicism shows the impatience of the new generation of young architects with Adam's Palladian grandeur. They no longer needed to go on the Grand Tour but only to the foot of the Mound or up Calton Hill to copy the pure, simple lines of the Parthenon. The west end of Royal Crescent was not completed until the 1880s, the plans being temporarily abandoned with the building of Scotland Street railway tunnel. The locked gate in the railings opposite originally was the 'gate' to the stands of St Bernard's Football Club, Edinburgh's lost team (*see Walk 8*).

Cross the foot of **Scotland Street**. The last house has a gate-pull as well as a set of bell-pulls beside the main door round the corner. This is an Edinburgh speciality much mocked by Glaswegians as a symptom of the capital's stand-offishness and lack of hospitality. If visitors did gain entry, it is claimed, they would be greeted by 'You'll have had your tea?'. Operated by wires and widely adopted in the New Town, bell pulls were the forerunner of the door answer phone.

Turn right up Scotland Street. The original naming of the streets in this area—Caledonia Street, Anglia Street, and Hibernia Street—celebrated the incorporation of Ireland into the United Kingdom in 1801, continuing the Unionist theme of the First New Town. In 1806 the names were changed to the less fanciful Scotland Street, London Street and Dublin Street respectively. Presumably Edinburgh Street was rejected!

At the top of Scotland Street, you reach **Drummond Place**, the square with a rounded end which balanced Royal Circus at the other end of the main axis of the Second New Town. Although the development of Drummond Place started in 1804, progress was slow until the end of the Napoleonic Wars. Building was not finally completed until 1823.

> **Drummond Place Gardens** were once the site of the country house belonging to Provost George Drummond, the driving force behind the creation of the New Town. He bought a small estate of thirteen acres here in 1757 and built Drummond Lodge for himself and his fourth wife. On his death, the estate was bought by General John Scott of Balcomie in Fife who replaced it with a much grander house, Bellevue. Scott was a famous gambler and, on his death, reputed to be the richest commoner in Scotland. His daughters married the Duke of Portland, the Earl of Moray and the Prime Minister, George Canning.
>
> The story goes that the house was paid for by Sir Laurence Dundas after Scott won Dundas's house in St Andrew Square at the gaming tables. Rather than give up his own house, Dundas agreed to build Scott a house to the latter's specification on Scott's estate. When Scott's widow died in 1802, the estate was bought by the Town Council and the house became the Excise Office. Unfortunately, it was undermined by the Scotland Street railway tunnel and demolished in 1845.

Over the years, Drummond Place has been home to the illustrious, the eccentric and the artistic. Charles Kirkpatrick Sharpe, a noted antiquary who fed Scott with incidents for his novels, lived at no 28 from 1835-51, having moved here from Princes Street. Noted for his eccentricity, his calling card bore a simple 'C#', a pun given additional point by its reference to his famously squeaky voice. Adam Black of the publishers A & C Black lived at no 38. Lord Provost from 1843-48, he made his fortune by purchasing the rights to publish Scott's novels and the *Encyclopaedia Britannica*. William McTaggart, the artist, lived at no 4, later bought by the brother of the architect Robert Lorimer, who remodelled it on his relative's behalf. Compton Mackenzie, the prolific twentieth-century writer and author of *Whisky Galore*, lived in numbers 31 and 32.

Turn left round the head of the Place, crossing London Street. A few doors along at no 15 London Street, a plaque commemorates one of Edinburgh's more surprising achievements, the Icelandic national anthem!

Continue round Drummond Place to turn left into **Dublin Street** and then right into Dublin Meuse, an unusual spelling. Continue into the picturesque Northumberland Place Lane. Here a coach house was adapted to form a chapel for the nuns of St David's Convent which occupied houses in Drummond Place up to the 1960s. A row of cottage-style houses in Nelson Place is followed by the traditional Star Tavern.

Cross and turn right down Nelson Street past the Polish Ex-Servicemen's Club, a reminder that many Poles emigrated to Scotland to escape Hitler and never left, to reach Drummond Place again.

Turn left into **Great King Street**. With its great width and houses designed in imposing blocks, this was planned to be the Second New Town's most prestigious address.

Unexpectedly, the houses were relatively slow to sell. Lacking garden views, Great King Street never quite achieved the cachet of Heriot Row or Moray Place.

Nonetheless, it is an impressive street with some distinguished former residents. J M Barrie, the author of *Peter Pan*, and Sir Robert Christison, the 'father of toxicology' and twice president of the Royal College of Physicians, both lived at no 3. More surprisingly, as he spent much of his life in abject poverty, Thomas de Quincey, author of *Confessions of an Opium Eater*, resided for a time at no 9.

On reaching **Dundas Street**, turn left up the hill with its art galleries and furniture restorers in the basements and its displays of fruit and vegetables on the street.

> On the left at 13A are the offices of the **New Town Conservation Committee.** Set up in 1970 as an outcome of a Conference of those concerned for the conservation of the New Town, the Committee has since master-minded the systematic restoration of the fabric of the area. It provides grants to assist with the often high costs of repairs to stonework, roofs and railings in appropriate materials and publishes a comprehensive manual on the care and restoration of Georgian houses. The office displays exhibitions on aspects of the New Town's history, development and conservation and sells a range of publications of local interest.

A few steps further up the hill return you to the start of the walk. Princes Street lies straight on, just over the summit.

Walk 4
EAST WINDY, WEST ENDY

The Western New Town

The walk starts by exploring the mix of old and new in the financial district round Rutland Square and the lively shopping streets of the West End. It then heads through the middle of the Western New Town, guided by the three spires of St Mary's Cathedral. A quiet stroll through the leafy crescents to the west is contrasted by some of the last streets to be developed in the New Town.

Introduction

With the core of the central New Town nearly complete, it was time to look east and west. At the same time as Regent Bridge was being built to mark the eastern gateway to the city, plans were drawn up for a grand entrance from the west. The main Glasgow Road was to be lined with terraces and crescents from the end of Princes Street to rural Haymarket.

In 1786, William Walker, an attorney in the Exchequer, purchased the land immediately to the west of Queensferry Street, the main route north, from the Easter Coates estate.

WALK 4

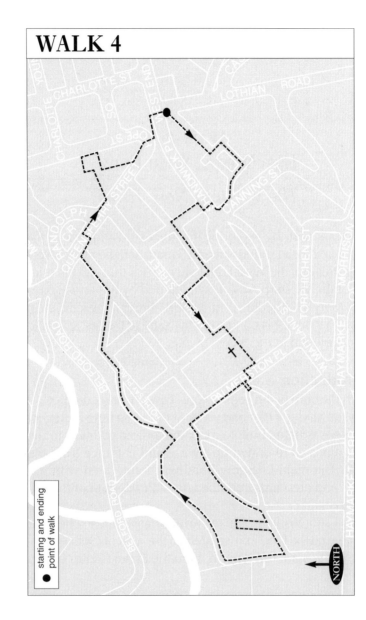

He wanted to give his son Patrick the title required to hold the ancient office of Usher of the White Rod dating back to the Scottish Parliament. The Walkers, the principal developers of the area, were joined by the trustees of James Erskine, Lord Alva, who owned the area round the street that bears his name.

As with the First and Second New Towns, the joint development plan involved a grand central street, Melville Street, in which the most prestigious houses would be set, with smaller, parallel streets to the north and south. Melville Street was to intersect with a major street running north-south, in the diamond-shaped square of Melville Crescent. Although this was designed as the focal point of the Walker development, it was thoroughly upstaged when Patrick Walker's daughters left their entire fortune to endow St Mary's Cathedral at the west end of Melville Street. Meanwhile, true crescents, Atholl and Coates, were being built on each side of the Glasgow road, while Rutland Square to the south was independently developed by John Learmonth.

Although Melville Street got off to a good start, overall development of the area was slow. Potential buyers of the grander houses preferred the greener ambience of the Moray Lands. Not until 1860 did Heriot's Trust have the confidence to lay out their lands in Wester Coates, to the west of the cathedral, in a series of the then fashionable crescents. These proved very popular with the professional classes—judges, advocates and surgeons. Where solid money moved, the private schools followed—St George's, St Denis's and Melville College, the latter founded as the

Edinburgh Institution in 1832 to teach modern languages, mathematics and science.

While today the crescents to the west remain largely residential, the Walker development has its fair share of financial and professional offices, although there is a growing trend to convert them back to houses once more.

Route

From the West End of Princes Street, cross over to the front of the imposing Caledonian Hotel whose sandstone frontage glows a deep terracotta when the sun is on it.

> **'The Caley'** was built in 1899 by the Caledonian Railway Company, whose Princes Street Station lay just behind. The aim was to rival the hotel at the other end of Princes Street above Waverley Station belonging to its competitor, the North British Railway Company. The two combatants ran well-publicised and hard-fought races to make the fastest time between London and Edinburgh, and on to Aberdeen.
>
> The five star Caley boasts 202 chimney pots and over two miles of carpeted corridor, which have cushioned the feet of monarchs, international leaders and stars of stage and screen. These have included Tommy Steele, Laurel and Hardy, Ginger Rogers and Sean Connery, a far cry from the days when 007 was a Co-op milkman from nearby Fountainbridge.

Turn into Rutland Street passing the neo-Norman church, formerly St Thomas Church of England, now more profanely a casino. At no 11, a plaque marks the home of Joseph

Lister, pioneer of antiseptic surgery. Opposite, the gates of Princes Street Station, closed in 1965, can still be seen.

Turn left into **Rutland Square**, an attractive setting for relatively small town houses with imposing porticoes, now largely given over to offices. At the next two corners of the square, you can catch a glimpse of Edinburgh's newest New Town. Like the First New Town, its promoters are public bodies, the City of Edinburgh Council and Lothian and Edinburgh Enterprise Ltd. The cluster of financial offices, hotels and the tall drum of the Edinburgh International Conference Centre has sprung up to the south in the last decade or so.

A bridge from the first corner leads into the imposing courtyard flanked by two wings of Standard Life, Europe's largest mutual insurance company. At the second corner are the headquarters of Baillie Gifford, the fund managers, with a spirited modern bronze statue 'Horse and Rider' by Eoghan Bridge. The monumental size of these modern developments contrasts with the essentially human and domestic scale of the earlier New Towns, however imposing they tried to be. They remind us that Edinburgh ranks fourth in Europe for the billions of pounds of other people's money it manages.

Continue round the Square past no 15, the offices of the Royal Incorporation of Architects in Scotland, which frequently hosts public exhibitions. Leave by the next corner, turning right into Canning Street to reach **Shandwick Place**. Looking left there is a view of the wide Atholl and Coates Crescents bracketing the road to Glasgow. These were among the first westward developments, Coates Crescent being started in 1813 and Atholl following in 1825. Atholl Crescent used to be the home of the Domestic Science College, or 'Dough School', now relocated to Queen Margaret College in Costorphine.

Turn right along Shandwick Place. Opposite is the fashionable church of St George's West, built in Baroque style in 1866 by David Bryce, with a later Venetian campanile by Rowand Anderson. Cross Shandwick Place at the lights, the pilot installation of 'speaking lights' for the blind, which have since been widely adopted.

Turn right and immediately left into **Stafford Street**. The imposing pillared frontage of the house at the end was designed to create an impressive vista from this point and, as the house of the Walker family, to be the best on the block. Stafford Street and neighbouring **William Street** are given over to speciality shops, takeaways, pubs and restaurants. You may want to pause here, as refreshment is scarce for the rest of the walk.

Go along William Street with its original Georgian shop fronts and turn right into **Walker Street**. Opposite just to the left, a stone plaque at no 8 commemorates the surgery of Elsie Inglis, the pioneering woman doctor and war heroine.

Turn right up Walker Street to reach the diamond-shaped square, perversely called **Melville Crescent**. In the centre stands a statue of the second Viscount Melville, MP for Midlothian from 1800, First Lord of the Admiralty and, continuing in his father's footsteps, manager of Tory electoral patronage in Scotland.

Although adjacent Melville Street sold well, being largely complete by 1825, there were few takers for the grand pillar-fronted houses of the 'Crescent', the centrepiece of the Walker development. Taste was moving away from show towards comfort and value for money. In 1855, a new architect was forced to produce a simpler design to get the sites let.

The development of the Walker Estate north of Melville Street proceeded very slowly, Chester Street, the northern equivalent of William Street being completed in the 1860s, Drumsheugh in the 1880s and Rothesay Terrace not until early the next century.

St Mary's Cathedral

Turn left into **Melville Street**, with its iron arches holding lamps over the wide front steps. The end is dominated by St Mary's Cathedral, its three spires visible from much of the city. St Mary's is by far the grandest church in Edinburgh, although it belongs to the Scottish Episcopal Church, very much a minority denomination, albeit one which has disproportionately wealthy congregations.

77

St Mary's Cathedral was the gift of the Walker sisters, daughters and heirs of Sir Patrick Walker, who left their entire fortune to the Episcopal Church for the purpose. Although the leading UK exponent of high Victorian Gothic, George Gilbert Scott, won the architectural competition held in 1872, St Mary's most distinctive feature, its three spires, was taken from another entry by Alexander Ross. The west spires are called Barbara and Mary after the Walker sisters.

The design is a composite of early Gothic with features taken from the Abbey of Holyrood, Jedburgh Abbey and Elgin Cathedral as well as churches in England and France. The overall effect, however, has a massiveness that is appropriately Scottish. As with the medieval cathedrals, building work went on for many years, from 1874 to 1917.

Cross Manor Place and take the road up the left side of the Cathedral: the Private Road sign bars only cars. Side-on, the Cathedral looks rather short for its height. On reaching **Palmerston Place**, opposite on your left is the former United Presbyterian Palmerston Place Church, built at the same time as the Cathedral but for a very different congregation and in a very different style.

Cross Palmerston Place at the traffic island and go a little way down to your right, noting for the first time the bay windows characteristic of the later 'Victorian' developments, although the dates by no means coincide with those of the Queen. The first two crescents to the left illustrate the transition well. Lansdowne Crescent has simple Georgian frontages while Grosvenor Crescent to the north has bay windows on all but the top storey. Yet Lansdowne Crescent was designed in 1861, when Victoria had already been

25 years on the throne, and Grosvenor only four years later. Traditional Edinburgh was slow to relinquish Georgian style for Victorian comfort.

Opposite is the west front of the Cathedral which, unlike most Edinburgh churches, is open seven days a week. Just beyond is Easter Coates House, the original house of the Coates estate and the city's oldest surviving dwelling outside the Old Town. It was built in 1615 for John Byres, a corn merchant with mills on the nearby Water of Leith. Embedded in the walls and gables of the much-extended house are medieval carvings taken from demolition sites in the Old Town. Since 1972 the building has housed St Mary's Music School, one of Scotland's schools for musically gifted children.

Cross the end of another pair of crescents and turn left. This form of layout was popular with later developers. It provided the desired outlook over gardens with the minimum use of ground, thus giving an efficient formula for converting land to money. Fork right into **Eglinton Crescent** to pass the German Consulate and one of the city's Youth Hostels. By the time these crescents were built in the 1870s bay windows were *de rigueur*. With its rich detailing and interiors, Eglinton Crescent reflects the Victorian taste for opulence. At the end of the Crescent, follow the pavement round to look into Magdala Mews, a pleasant, out of the way corner. Carry on as the road bends round into **Magdala Crescent**.

The name is very much a product of the Crescent's date of building, 1869. In the previous year, Lord Napier took the

Donaldson's Hospital

mountain stronghold of the Emperor Theodore of Abyssinia at Magdala in a daring raid, a feat for which he was awarded the freedom of the city. The exploit raised great imperial fervour, prompting the naming of this pleasant line of villas with their rather top-heavy dormer windows.

Magdala Crescent overlooks the grounds of **Donaldson's Hospital**, a truly palatial school for the deaf. Funded by the legacy of James Donaldson of Broughton Hall, a prosperous printer in the Old Town's West Bow who died in 1830, it was designed by Playfair in a grand and correct Elizabethan style. Built between 1842 and 1851, it was opened by Queen Victoria. She admired it greatly, allegedly offering to swap Holyrood Palace for it as her Scottish residence! In more recent times, it was suggested more than once as a potential home for the Scottish Parliament, perhaps because of a certain resemblance to the Palace of Westminster.

Continue along Magdala Crescent to reach Douglas Crescent which overlooks the steep wooded valley of the Water of Leith. A path runs down from the corner to the Water of Leith Walkway and Dean Village (*see Walk 6*). At the end of Douglas Crescent, the smaller scale of this almost suburban area is broken by a seven-storey block facing you across Palmerston Place. The road falls steeply away down the hill to Belford Bridge over the Water of Leith.

Cross the busy Palmerston Place, turning right and first left into **Rothesay Terrace**. Although Rothesay Terrace—actually a crescent just to confuse—was the last part of the Western New Town to be completed, its style remains consistent with the rest. The one exception is no 3, the Jacobean-style residence of John R Findlay, proprietor of the *Scotsman* and philanthropist. From his back windows he could see the results of his philanthropy, the picturesque housing of Well Court in Dean Village which he had endowed (*see Walk 6*).

Continue in the same direction, as Rothesay Terrace becomes a side of the triangular **Drumsheugh Gardens**, another late development dating from 1874-1882. Opposite the houses have rather stark, rectangular bay windows, a style which did not catch on. As Drumsheugh Gardens turns towards **Queensferry Street**, note the elaborately-paved basement area of no 19 with seat and silver fountain. Facing you is one of the (fortunately few) total intrusions on the New Town streetscape, the 1950s Meldrum House, which replaced St Andrew's Free church.

Cross Queensferry Street at the lights, and turn right and then second left into Randolph Place. At the head of this cobbled cul-de-sac there is a mock-Tudor, half-timbered building, quite unexpected in this northern city. You may wish to go round the front of West Register House on Charlotte Square to compare its Georgian grandeur with the Victorian terraces you have just seen.

Turn right down Queensferry Lane to return to the West End of Princes Street and the start of the walk.

Walk 5
GRANDEUR AND GREENERY

The Moray Estate and the Water of Leith

After exploring the Moray Estate, the grandest and most successful of the New Town developments, the walk winds down the hill by mews and back lanes to the least fashionable part of the Raeburn Estate. It returns through the valley of the Water of Leith, passing a Greek temple, two mineral wells and a baronial squash court and going under the high arches of Dean Bridge.

Introduction

During the building of the First New Town, workers used to catch rabbits for lunch in the Earl of Moray's Parks. His lands lay above the Water of Leith to the north west of the First New Town. At first he resisted the upstart New Town. The Town Council had to come to terms with the Earl in order to complete Charlotte Square as planned. The boundary of his estate can still be traced as it cuts diagonally through the back gardens of the north side of the Square.

By 1820, the First New Town was virtually complete and the Second well under way. Work had started on the

WALK 5

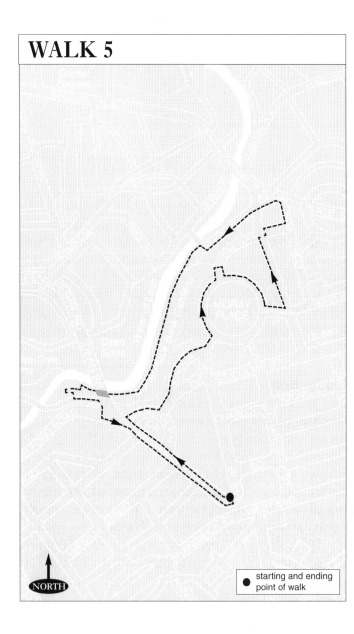

NORTH

● starting and ending
point of walk

Western New Town and on the Raeburn Estate across the Water of Leith. Finding his estate about to be engulfed by the city, the Earl of Moray decided to cash in on the boom. In 1822, he commissioned James Gillespie Graham to draw up plans for the development of his land.

A relatively narrow strip sloping steeply down towards the river bank, it was not an easy site on which to fit a classical layout. Gillespie Graham rose to the challenge. The design he produced was not only a commercial success but, with its interconnected crescent, ellipse and dodecagon, a superlative architectural composition.

The speed at which the property was feued is the more surprising considering the stringent conditions, both financial and architectural, which the Earl imposed on feuars. These applied not only to the houses but also to the stable blocks and outbuildings. The feuars were responsible for virtually everything, including the provision of roads and services, while the Earl stipulated the design in fine detail. He took one of the finest houses for himself, sat back and waited for the rents to roll in. Whatever his motives, he left a remarkable architectural legacy.

Route

Start from the West End of Princes Street, under the 'By Royal Appointment' Arms at the entrance to Fraser's department store. This was known for generations as 'Binn's corner' a popular meeting place for Edinburgh ladies on shopping expeditions.

Cross Queensferry Street at the lights and go along it,

crossing both ends of **Randolph Crescent**. The Earl of Moray had originally intended to build a house for himself in the middle of the gardens but later decided that Moray Place was sufficiently to his taste. The end of Queensferry Street is marked by the high and imposing tenement of Randolph Cliff, one of the last parts of the Moray Estate to be built about 1850. Perched over a sheer drop, it has spectacular views over Dean Bridge and the river valley.

Turn right into Randolph Crescent with its giant Doric pilasters, a more typical example of Gillespie Graham's grand but nonetheless practical designs. Steell, the sculptor, had his studio at no 9.

Turn left into **Great Stuart Street**. At no 17, first William Playfair, who gave the New Town much of its classical grandeur, and then Sir Robert Lorimer, the leading Scottish arts and crafts designer, had their architectural practices. Great Stuart Street leads into **Ainslie Place** where two crescents face each other across gardens, forming an ellipse. Here, as elsewhere in the New Town, residents have taken advantage of the wide basement areas to create their own gardens in tubs and containers.

At the end of Ainslie Place, you rejoin Great Stuart Street, a layout calculated to confuse, before reaching **Moray Place**. First impressions are of sheer size and scale. Moray Place forms a dodecagon, or twelve-sided space, nearly 200 yards across. The corner and centre pavilions are fronted by rows of up to six columns, giving an effect that if anything is even grander than Adam's Charlotte Square. Many of the houses have access not only to the central

Moray Place

area but also to private gardens behind on the slopes leading down to the Water of Leith.

Turn left to go round Moray Place past the Earl's own house at no 28. Look down Doune Terrace, built on the slope descending to Stockbridge with extensive views over north west Edinburgh. The steepness of the terrain has meant that some of the houses have two basements. Windows in the lower basements are almost buried underground, in one case no more than a grilled space under the doorstep.

Continue round Moray Place to reach **Darnaway Street** and turn left. The first house on each side has dummy windows painted in. Although not required on a corner frontage, they maintain the symmetry of the facade.

Turn left down **Gloucester Lane**, a pleasant mews. This used to be known as Church Lane, being the route from the village of Stockbridge to St Cuthbert's, the parish church for the whole of the New Town. Numbers 18 and 19 open off an outside stair while no 20 has a semi-detached residence for birds. On the left about half way down is Gloucester Square, a mews courtyard overshadowed by the high backs of Moray Place behind.

On reaching **Gloucester Place**, you move from the Moray Lands back into the Second New Town. Cross and turn right past no 6, the home of John Wilson, Professor of Moral Philosophy at Edinburgh University. Under the *nom de plume* 'Christopher North', he was a well-known literary character and contemporary of Sir Walter Scott.

Turn left into India Street and take the flight of steps on the left leading down under the forestairs of the houses on the steep hill past two basement levels and some ingenious car parking to reach North West Circus Place. Turn left and left again into **India Place**. A modern block on the left is contrasted with two rubble-built eighteenth-century houses on the right.

The painter, David Roberts, was born in the second house, known as **Duncan's Land**, in 1796. The son of a shoemaker, he started out as a scene painter in a circus, working his way up to a more exalted position in the Drury Lane Theatre, London. He then went on his artistic travels which resulted in paintings of Spanish, Italian and Middle Eastern scenes. Prints of these paintings hung in many a Victorian drawing room.

The stone above the door with the inscription FEAR GOD ONLYE 1605 IR is thought to come from a house in the Lawnmarket. Duncan's Land is now a branch of the international restaurant chain, Pierre Victoire, founded and headquartered in the city.

Carry on along India Place or, if you are feeling adventurous, take the following detour. Turn left and go a little way up Gloucester Lane and then turn right into the Stockbridge Health Centre car park. At the far end there is a slightly overgrown path through a bank of scrubby woodland running beneath the retaining wall of Doune Terrace. Follow it for about thirty yards before taking a wooden flight of steps back down to India Place.

> **India Place** and the parallel Saunders Street running along the riverside were built as rows of high, plain, working-class tenements by the developers of the Raeburn Estate across the river (*see Walk 7*). By the 1960s, India Place had fallen into disrepair and had an unenviable reputation as a rough and grimy area. This reputation, however, did not extend to neighbouring Saunders Street with its thriving, respectable community and Fire Station. In the spirit of the times and in the cause of slum clearance, both streets were swept away. The inhabitants were rehoused for the most part in Muirhouse—an area whose reputation is now much like that which India Place used to have. The blocks of housing which replaced them, set at right angles to the river, somehow lack the character of the old tenements.

As you go along India Place, note the coal cellars or air raid shelters of the former tenements in the bank on the left. At the end of the street, a single villa, built around 1800, is a reminder of Stockbridge before the incursion of the Raeburn development changed its character from rural to urban almost overnight.

Turn right to reach Mackenzie Bridge across the Water of Leith. Do not cross the bridge but take the impressively wide steps on the left leading down to a stone balustraded walkway along the side of the river. A few yards on you come to a domed and pillared classical temple by the waterside.

When a mineral spring was discovered here in 1760, at a time when mineral waters were seen as the cure for all ills, it was christened **St Bernard's Well** and enclosed in a simple well house. In 1788, the well was bought by Lord Gardenstone, an Edinburgh judge and noted eccentric. He shared his room with his pet pigs and his bed with their piglets. Maybe his prodigious consumption of snuff was to avoid the smell.

Lord Gardenstone commissioned Alexander Naysmith, the landscape painter, to design a temple over the well dedicated to Hygeia, the goddess of health. Her statue stands under the dome. He appointed a custodian and set regulations for the consumption of the suitably foul-tasting water, sold to adults at one penny a glass and to children at half price. Consumers were instructed to take a brisk walk of at least five minutes after taking the waters and not to hang about the well, a stipulation designed not only for their welfare but to make way for other customers.

The well was bought by the Edinburgh publisher, Thomas Nelson, in 1885. He restored and donated it as a gift to the city three years later as the plaque at the foot of the steps records. The motto on the pump room pedestal: BIBENDO VALERIS—drink and you will be well—turned out not to be true. The well was finally closed in 1956 on suspicion that the water might be contaminated. The restored building is occasionally open to the public.

Take the steps up the side of the well to join the higher path above the river with the gardens of the Moray Lands rising steeply on your left. The path forms part of the **Water of Leith Walkway**, which runs from Balerno, to the west of the city, to the mouth of the river at Leith. Developed over many years by the Water of Leith Walkway Trust, it recently received a Millennium award to fund improvements and to open a visitor centre at Slateford, midway along the route. Walks 6, 7 and 8 cover other sections of this unusual means of crossing the city.

A little further on, a small stone shed houses St George's Well, a mineral spring which never achieved the fame of St Bernard's. Here, the gorge is at its deepest, and, after

St Bernard's Well

91

rain, the river sets up a good roar as it rushes over the stony bottom. Once heavily polluted by the paper mills upstream, the Water of Leith is now pure enough to support trout. There have even been sightings of otters surprisingly close to the city centre.

Rounding a corner, you suddenly come upon the arches of Dean Bridge soaring high above.

As early as 1825, John Learmonth, the owner of the Dean Estate on the north bank of the river, decided to jump on the New Town bandwagon and develop his land, commissioning plans from James Jardine and Gillespie Graham. He proposed building **Dean Bridge** to provide the necessary access, intending to recoup the cost from the profits made by feuing his land. The Cramond Turnpike Trustees, responsible for the upkeep of the public road beyond the river, agreed to share the costs on condition that the leading Scottish engineer, Thomas Telford, was employed to design the bridge.

It was a wise stipulation. Functional, elegant and virtually unaltered, Dean Bridge stands thirty-two metres high with a four-arch span of 138 metres now carrying the traffic of one of the main roads out of the city. It was not, however, a profitable speculation for John Learmonth. The development boom passed with little of his land feued and he eventually had to sell out to the Heriot Trust.

The curious castellated building on your left after the bridge was built in 1913 as a squash court; hence its lack of windows. This part of the river, known as Miller Row, was once lined with mills powered by the water of the river.

Take the flight of steps up through the car park of the architects, RMJM Scotland, to reach **Bell's Brae**, and turn left up the steep slope. There are seats on the left about half way for those in need of a rest. At the top, Kirkbrae House used to be a tavern, allowing the Baxters to slake their thirst on their way home from the dusty mills (*see Walk 6*).

Turn right, crossing Belford Road, to return to Queensferry Street. As you go up it there are fine views along the broad streets of the Western New Town towards St Mary's Cathedral. David Brewster, inventor of the kaleidoscope and editor of the *Encyclopaedia Britannica*, lived at no 1 Melville Street. Just before reaching the west end of Princes Street and the end of the walk, you pass Mather's Bar, opened in 1902 by the Edinburgh spirit merchant, Hugh Mather. With its wooden floor and pedimented bar fittings, it retains the atmosphere of spit and sawdust typical of Scottish pubs in the days of hard drinking and a male-only clientele.

WALK 6

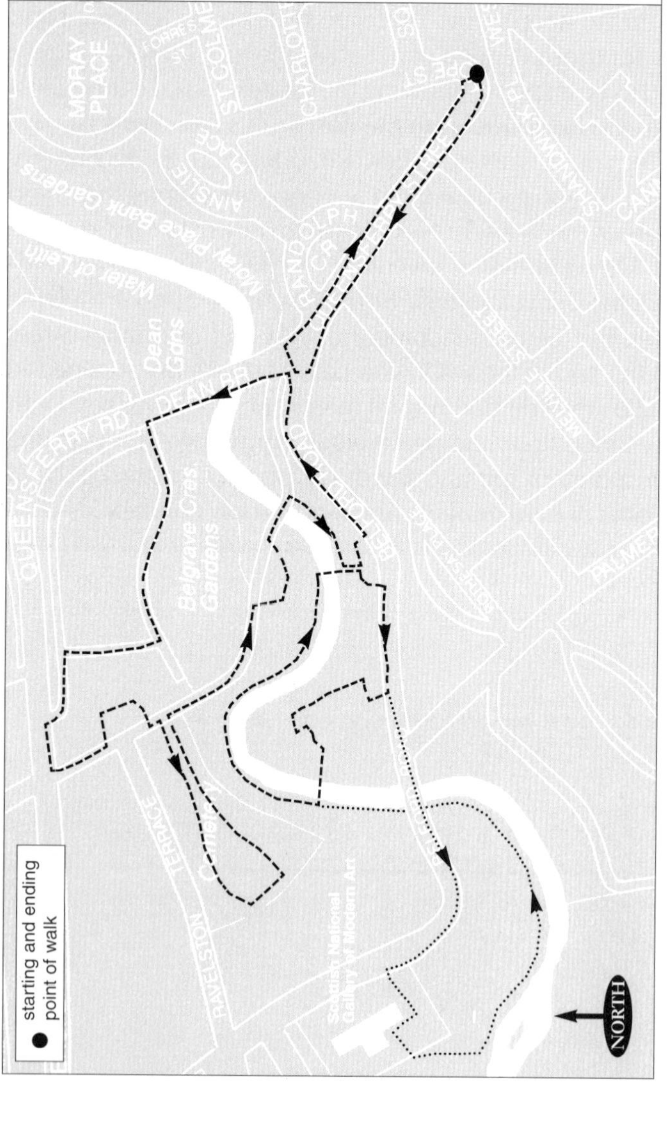

NORTH

● starting and ending
point of walk

MORAY PLACE

FORRES ST

ST COLME ST

CHARLOTTE SQ

WEST

PE ST

SHANDWICK PL

AINSLIE PLACE

Moray Place Bank Gardens

Water of Leith

Dean Gdns

RANDOLPH CR

MELVILLE STREET

DEAN BR

QUEENSFERRY RD

Belgrave Cres.
Gardens

FORRES RD

PALMER

RAVELSTON TERRACE

Scottish National
Gallery of Modern Art

Walk 6
A City Gorge

Dean Village and the Water of Leith

The walk crosses the Dean Bridge to explore a late but attractive outlier of the New Town and a Victorian cemetery where many distinguished residents found their final resting place. A descent to the picturesque Dean Village is followed by a visit to the former industrial enclave of Sunbury and a walk along the wooded banks of the Water of Leith. There is an optional extension to take in the Scottish National Gallery of Modern Art.

Note: once you leave Queensferry Street, there is no chance of a cup of coffee or something stronger on this route until you reach the Gallery of Modern Art.

Introduction

For a great European city, Edinburgh has a very modest river. The Water of Leith circles the west and north sides of the New Town on its eight-mile journey to the Forth. At the foot of a steep-sided gorge, carved out by the river, was Water of Leith Village, whose mills provided the City's Incorporation of Baxters (bakers) with flour.

The smaller village of Dean perched on top of the ridge across the valley, at the gates of Dean House. When the hamlet was largely demolished to build Belgrave Mews, the name Dean was co-opted for the village in the valley. Although Water of Leith village was referred to as Dean as early as the opening of Bell Court in 1886, it was not until the 1920s that the renaming was officially recognised in the Post Office Directory.

The valley formed a north-west barrier to the expanding city. It was crossed by a narrow bridge, necessitating a steep climb down and up again. John Learmonth, the owner of the lands immediately to the north, promoted and largely financed the high level Dean Bridge across the ravine, designed by Thomas Telford and opened in 1831 (*see box, Walk 5*).

Although it took another twenty years for residential development to spread to the far side of the bridge, institutions were quicker off the mark. The building, in 1825, of John Watson's Hospital, a charity boarding school for fatherless children of the professional classes, was followed by the Dean Orphanage in 1833, Dean Cemetery in 1845 and Daniel Stewart's College in 1848.

Dean Village remained a flourishing milling centre until the latter part of the nineteenth century, when it lost out to the large, steam-driven mills in Leith which could take advantage of direct shipments of grain through the port. In 1883 philanthropic and aesthetic motives combined to replace much of the depressed village with the well-built and consciously picturesque housing that remains today.

Despite the demise of the mills, the village retained its

industrial character with a tannery occupying a site by the river until the 1970s. With an eye for an opportunity just like Learmonth before them, the property developers then moved in.

Route

From the west end of Princes Street, walk out along Queensferry Street, crossing narrow Queensferry Street Lane and Alva Street flying the flag of European Union outside the European Commission's office. You then cross Melville Street, set against the backdrop of the east end of St Mary's Cathedral, and Drumsheugh Gardens. Keep straight on as Queensferry Street becomes Lynedoch Place. Designed by James Milne in 1820, the houses here have long front gardens mirroring his Ann Street design on the Raeburn Estate (*see Walk 7*).

Dean Bridge

Cross Belford Road and Bells Brae to fork right onto **Dean Bridge**. On the left stands Kirkbrae House. Now much modified, in the eighteenth century it functioned as a tavern serving the bakers and millers of Dean Village. You can see their arms and a cube-shaped sundial on the wall as well as carved stones from Dean House, demolished in 1845. On the right, the high tenements of Randolph Cliff perch right on the edge of the valley.

From the Bridge, there are spectacular views in both directions, somewhat obscured by the high parapets. These were raised in 1912 to deter would-be suicides who found the sheer drop to the river below compelling. To the left are the rooftops, both ancient and modern, of Dean Village with the converted mill prominent by the river. To the right, the backs of the houses on the Moray Lands (*see Walk 5*) line the valley's edge with the tower blocks of Leith in the far distance.

The Perpendicular **Holy Trinity Episcopal Church** of 1837 is a prominent landmark on the far side of Dean Bridge. Although designed by John Henderson, it closely resembles William Burn's Church of St John at the west end of Princes Street. With three Episcopal churches including St Mary's Cathedral within less than half a mile, it is perhaps not surprising that Holy Trinity was declared surplus to requirements in 1957.

For the next twenty years, while continuing to look like a church, it was in fact an electricity substation, a highly imaginative use of a redundant building. In 1988, Christian Centre Missionaries bought the building and rebuilt the gutted interior entirely by voluntary effort and funding. It is now once more a church, a rare reversal of the usual trend.

Turn left down the side of the Church into **Belgrave Crescent**. At first, the Crescent hugs the valley's edge with glimpses of the river and a weir below, but it soon curves back to make room for private gardens. Built as late as 1874, the houses make the most of the open outlook with large bay windows and rows of attic dormers.

Near the end of Belgrave Crescent, turn right into Belgrave Place and then left into Buckingham Terrace. This takes you back to Queensferry Road. There is a view opposite to the Gothic spire of Fettes College, designed in 1864 by David Bryce in Scots Baronial style. Established as an educational institution through the charity of the Edinburgh merchant and underwriter, Sir William Fettes, it is now a leading boarding school and the *alma mater* of Prime Minister Tony Blair. To its left is the blue cylinder of Granton Gas Works.

Turn left past the sombre 1930s Bristo Baptist Church and left again up Dean Path. Turn left into Belgrave Mews, a pleasant lane that occupies the site of the former Dean Village. On regaining Dean Path, cross to the main entrance of **Dean Cemetery**. It was laid out in 1845 in the grounds of Dean House, seat of the Nisbets of Dean, which was demolished to make way for the cemetery.

Go up the main avenue between the suitably solemn lines of yew and holly. At the grass circle, take the path diagonally left and then right at the junction. On your right just before the first path to the right, there is the monument

Dean Cemetery

to Sam Bough, the Victorian painter, with his brushes and palette in bronze at its base. Continue down the mossy path to the end wall past a large memorial to those killed in the Crimean War.

Close to the wall stands a striking pyramid designed by Playfair with a sculptured portrait of its incumbents, Lord Rutherford and his wife, by John Steell. To the left, two of the most prominent figures in the history of Edinburgh's New Town lie side by side. William Playfair, its leading architect, has a plain classical monument while Lord Cockburn, its chronicler, lies under flamboyant Gothic arches.

Over the cemetery wall stands the former **Dean Orphanage**, built in 1831 to a design by Thomas Hamilton. An orphanage overlooking a graveyard is a poignant although unintentional juxtaposition. One zealous Superintendent managed to double the intake of inmates. The facade of the Orphanage incorporates a clock-face salvaged from

100

the Netherbow Port, one of the gates in the medieval city walls. On the roof are two strange open-work towers.

The building is currently being converted by the National Galleries of Scotland to house the works of Scotland's leading sculptor, Sir Eduardo Paolozzi, born in Leith of Italian extraction. One of his works can be seen in the grounds of the Gallery of Modern Art and another in Picardy Place (*see Walk 9*). The new gallery is expected to open in spring, 1999.

Continue to your left along the path taking first left at the large Waddell tomb and forking right at the memorial to John Wilson, 'Scottish vocalist'. Born in the Canongate in 1800, he was a noted tenor of his time, giving a command performance for Queen Victoria. He died of cholera while on tour in America.

Go to the next crossing. On your right is a bizarre monument to John Leishman, three winged lions supporting rams' heads topped by three cranes or pelicans. Opposite and a little to the right lies Robert Reid, the architect of Heriot Row and much more besides, although his reputation has suffered by comparison with his greater contemporary, Robert Adam.

You may wish to spend longer exploring the record of the lives of the illustrious, the respectable and the curious who once walked the New Town's streets, including the pioneer of photography, David Octavius Hill, and James Buchanan, the Glasgow magnate lying under the weightiest monument of all. To find your way back to the main gate, turn left at the Leishman monument. Follow the path until you come to a flight of steps down to the right. This takes you along a terrace overlooking the river with carvings from the seventeenth-century Dean House set in the retaining wall, before climbing up again to reach the main gate.

On leaving the Cemetery, turn right down the hill past old houses and modern infill to reach **Dean Path Buildings** with their red sandstone window surrounds. Take the steps through the buildings. This is Convening Court, where at one time the local trades may have met.

At the foot you arrive in Damside, a modern development of ochre-harled flats on the site of the former tannery. Turn left to reach **Well Court**, built along with Dean Path Buildings by John Findlay, the proprietor of the *Scotsman* newspaper, in 1883-86. His motives were mixed. Not only did he wish, as public benefactor, to improve the housing conditions of the poor, but also, as local resident, to provide a more picturesque view from his house on the heights of Rothesay Terrace. The courtyard contains the traditional washing lines still in use. The picturesque clock tower in the corner over a meeting hall for tenants now houses a lighting design business.

Continue to the foot of Dean Path. Opposite stands the imposing former West Mill, built in the early nineteenth century and now converted into flats. It was powered by two water wheels, each eighteen feet in diameter and twelve feet wide. The arches which housed the wheels can be seen above the water line.

Turn right past the former school, identifiable by the sculptured roundel on the gable—'Edinburgh School Board, 1875' and 'Education'—to reach the eighteenth-century bridge over the river. From here there is a view back to Holy Trinity Church and the towering Dean Bridge. At the head of the bridge stands the former granary of the Incorporation of Baxters, decorated with their sculptured arms and a barely legible inscription below a small shuttered window.

GOD BLESS THE BAXTERS OF EDIN
BRUGH UHO BULT THIS HOUS 1675

Turn right into **Hawthornbank Lane**, passing the large gable window of Drumsheugh Baths and a pleasant row of houses of various dates. The road narrows and leads down to the riverside, looking across to Well Court with its large oriel windows. Follow the road round under the archways of the self-consciously picturesque modern housing, up the hill and round to the right to reach Belford Road.

Pass a newsagent where you can buy a history of Dean Village. After turning right into Sunbury Street, take first right and then left into **Belford Mews**. On the left is a row of artisan housing of about 1865 while on the right lower down is a modern interpretation of mews houses fronted by bold helmeted turrets. At the end, turn left past Sunbury House, the premises of the old established interior furnishers and Royal Warrant-holders, Whytock and Reid. Next door is Belford Lodge, a modern house with palm trees among its well-tended lawns.

For a detour to take in the Scottish National Gallery of Modern Art consult the final paragraphs of this walk. Otherwise, turn up Sunbury Street, lined with small mews houses, and take the flight of steps down to the right into a large modern development of brick town houses. Go slightly left and right to find, facing you at the end of the development, an inconspicuous right of way between two blocks of housing (between nos 15 and 16) which leads to a narrow bridge over the river.

Turn right and follow the path through a wooded gorge by the river. At the entrance to Dean Village the path turns into a metal platform built out over the ten-foot high weir that once provided the power for the Dean Village mills. The roar of falling water immediately beneath one's feet can be disconcerting experience. A few yards further on, the river is crossed by a foot-bridge. Go under the bridge and then turn sharply left to cross it.

Pass under the modern archway again. This time, turn left into what appears at first sight to be a garage forecourt and take the flight of steps leading up from the end. At the top, turn left past some older houses to join Belford Road.

Pass the front of the private Drumsheugh Baths, the grilles outside echoing the Moorish interior. As you head towards Queensferry Street, there are final views across the roofs of Dean Village. The last house on the left has the inscription 'Drumsheugh Toll' above the door, taken from an earlier building on the site.

Turn right on to Queensferry Street to return to the West End and the start of the walk.

Taking in the Gallery of Modern Art

Ignoring the steps down, continue along Sunbury Street to reach Belford Road, turning right to cross **Belford Bridge**.

Opposite is the Hilton National Hotel on the site of the former Bell's Mills. One of the mill buildings can still be seen by the riverside.

Go up the hill and turn into the main gate of the Scottish National Gallery of Modern Art. William Burn's plain classical building of 1825 was formerly John Watson's School. The grounds are the setting for works of art. At the foot of the drive is a kinetic sculpture, two moving fingers slowly pointing to the sky, while at the head of the drive sits Paolozzi's 'Architect of the Universe', inspired by Blake's famous engraving. The Gallery is well worth a visit: admission is free although there may be a charge for special exhibitions. There is also a shop and a tearoom with tables in the garden in summer.

Go round to the left of the Gallery through the car park. A gap in the back wall leads to a path zigzagging down to a bridge across the Water of Leith. Here, the valley starts to open out. Across the river, turn left. You may hear the sound of tennis balls from the courts of the Edinburgh Sports Club opposite. Passing through a wall the path forms a platform built out over the river before crossing over a footbridge to pass behind the Hilton Hotel and under Belford Bridge to rejoin the walk.

WALK 7

NORTH

● starting and ending
point of walk

Walk 7

Stockaree

Stockbridge and the Raeburn Estate

This walk explores the village of Stockbridge. Each of its three loops, taking in the area round St Stephen Street, the Raeburn Estate and Raeburn Place, and the riverside, starts close to the bridge over the Water of Leith.

After a bohemian shopping street and an elegant mews, you come on the rural serenity of the Raeburn Estate on the opposite slope of the valley. Returning down Stockbridge's main street, you head along the Water of Leith to visit a pioneering housing co-operative and the tranquil square where Stockbridge meets the city.

Introduction

The widening of the valley of the Water of Leith, as it leaves the gorge in which Dean Village nestles, provided a convenient ford across which cattle driven from the North reached the city markets in Broughton and the Old Town. A small village grew up round the river crossing, bridged in the seventeenth century, while the mansions and grounds of Deanhaugh and St Bernard's looked down from their heights across the river.

In 1789, the lands of Deanhaugh to the north west were acquired by the painter Henry Raeburn, through his marriage to Ann, the widow of James Leslie of Deanhaugh. In 1813 a start was made to his development, replacing the houses of the local gentry with neat Georgian terraces, lighter in style than the rest of the New Town.

Following the line of the old drove road and turnpike, Raeburn Place, named after the painter, is the main shopping street of Stockbridge. Although the original village extended along the banks of the river, from the middle of the nineteenth century onwards the rural dwellings were engulfed by industry and working class tenements. Life in Stockbridge could be tough but never dull!

Today, the impression of a living local community remains strong, although workshops have given way to modern flats and the pawnbroker to the antique shop. With lower house prices than much of the New Town, Stockbridge is popular with young people. Judging by the number of sheltered housing developments, it also appeals to older people, both former residents who were moved away during the slum clearances of the 1960s and those who once lived further up the hill but now value life on the level.

Route

The walk starts from the bridge at Stockbridge. It can be reached from Princes Street by taking the no 28 bus from the Mound, or by walking down via Frederick Street, Howe Street, Circus Place and Granville Place.

Stand at the corner of **Hamilton Place** and **Granville Place**. Here is the hub of the nineteenth century village. The two towers ahead were once the church and the bank. The larger tower on your left, incorporated into a sheltered housing development, is all that remains of Stockbridge Free Church. It has led a charmed life, having been moved in 1867 from Lothian Road when its site was needed for a railway station. The pizza parlour with its terrace overhanging the river was built as a branch of Edinburgh Savings Bank.

Turn right into Hamilton Place and you will find some other essential features of community life. The public convenience backing rather inauspiciously onto the river was the fire station until 1906 while its neighbour to the right was the police station. Nineteenth-century Edinburgh had a policy of putting its emergency services in one place.

Take the first turning on the right under the arch into **St Stephen Place**. A washing green and trees fill a courtyard between traditional tenements built in the 1840s and Mill House, a modern housing association scheme. The courtyard is on the site of Stockbridge Market, the first outside the Old Town. Opened in 1826, the market survived into the twentieth century, although on a diminished scale after the building of St Stephen Place over much of its ground. Leave by the other entrance arch to the market with its vestiges of an ironwork canopy and its inscription promising 'Butcher meat, fruits, fish and poultry'.

Turn left into **St Stephen Street**. Started in 1824 from the east end adjacent to the burgeoning New Town, it was originally called Brunswick Street but was renamed three years later when St Stephen's church was built. With its double-decker rows of shops, selling a rich trove of merchandise from antique lamp fittings to designer knitwear, and its slightly alternative cafes, exploring St Stephen Street makes a pleasant diversion on the walk.

Follow the street round, passing on the opposite side a red brick church hall and a school, now a school of theatre and dance and flats respectively, to reach the monumental St Stephen's Church (*see Walk 3*). There are views to the 'new town' of Silvermills springing up in the valley. Across the road is the much more modest, neo-gothic, Episcopalian Collegiate Church of St Vincent. It also has the imposing designation of the Church of the Military and Hospitaller Order of St Lazarus of Jerusalem Grand Commandery of Lochore.

Cross and go round St Vincent's Church to turn right into **Circus Lane**, a wide and elegant mews with shrubs in neat tubs outside the doors. It curves to the left, following the line of the houses of Royal Circus.

Turn right down North West Circus Place, Kerr Street and Granville Place to return to the bridge. Different names for short stretches of the same street are designed to confuse the unwary. The confusion is added to by the use of the black and gold Stockbridge signs, indicating an area of historic interest.

Cross the main road at the lights, then carry on over the bridge, built at the turn of the century to replace the original stone bridge of 1786 and its wooden (stock) predecessor. You are now entering the Raeburn Estate.

Henry Raeburn, one of the greatest portrait painters of all time, was born in Stockbridge in 1756. His father was a yarn-boiler on the banks of the Water of Leith. Orphaned when young, Henry attended George Heriot's School while his elder brother carried on the business. At 16, Raeburn was apprenticed to a goldsmith, no doubt in recognition of his artistic aptitude. It is not known how he moved on to portraiture; possibly through the related trade of painting miniatures.

In 1780, he married his neighbour, Ann Leslie, of Deanhaugh House, a widow eleven years his senior. It was a good marriage. Raeburn acquired not only a loving wife but also two step-daughters, social standing and the Deanhaugh Estate. He went on to buy the adjacent and larger St Bernard's House to reflect his growing status.

Although his painting career prospered, other business ventures were less successful. In 1808, Raeburn was faced with bankruptcy, paying his debts only with the greatest difficulty, although he managed to hold on to his house and land. In 1813 he started to feu the land for building, starting with Ann Street, named after his wife.

His paintings, including a self-portrait, can be seen at the Scottish National Portrait Gallery and the National Gallery of Scotland, whose trademark is Raeburn's 'Skating Minister' as well as in galleries and stately homes throughout the UK. He was knighted on the occasion of George IV's visit to Edinburgh in 1822, but died the following year.

Turn left along **Dean Terrace**, passing on your left one of Edinburgh's blue former police boxes and, across the river, the ends of the Saunders Street flats, replacing the earlier tenement slums. Dean Terrace was originally Mineral Street, a reference to the mineral waters of St Bernard's Well (*see Walk 5*).

Turn right up Carlton Street, with its delicate cast iron balconies characteristic of the area, to reach the double-sided oval of **St Bernard's Crescent**. This is the New Town at its most flamboyant. Its design supposedly inspired by the painter, Sir David Wilkie, the rows of bold Doric pillars and horizontal lines of St Bernard's Crescent give it a more imposing and weighty feel than the rest of the development. Raeburn's home, St Bernard's House, had to be demolished to make way for the Crescent, designed by James Milne in 1824, two years after the painter's death. To the right, Leslie Place was not built until the 1880s, the owner of Deanhaugh House being less enthusiastic than his neighbours to cash in on the building boom.

Cross Leslie Place to go round the Crescent, admiring the restrained wealth of the interiors—glowing mahogany, chandeliers and heavy window drapes. Cross back where the road narrows to return along the less complete side. Money was a perennial problem in finishing the project, resulting in isolated blocks adopting the original design interspersed with later infill.

Turn right into **Danube Street** whose gentle curve flows into a straight run down to the river. With its continuous line of balconies, the elegance of Danube Street is only marred by the slightly ungainly joins between its central blocks and their flanking terraces. Until the 1980s, Danube Street had a certain unexpected notoriety, as home of a high-class brothel run by the colourful Dora Noyce. Preferring to describe it as 'more of a YMCA with extras', she served tea in a silver pot to visitors while they waited to go upstairs. The end of the street looks across the river to the backs of Moray Place perched on the cliff edge.

Turn right into Upper Dean Terrace. In winter, you can see the colonnaded temple of St Bernard's Well through the trees at the far end. As you round the corner, the exquisite Georgian jewel of **Ann Street** gradually unfolds. Unusually for the time, each house is set behind its own front garden, making Ann Street one of the most sought-after addresses in the city. The first part of the Raeburn estate to be developed, the houses are in fact quite small, with very little servant accommodation and no space for carriages. It is conjectured that they were built for letting to visitors to the city, on the model of Bath. Raeburn himself may have designed the street frontages, while James Milne laid out the interiors to the specification of individual buyers. Legend has it that Milne owned the bow-windowed no 35, the only house to depart from the prescribed facade.

Make your way down the left hand side of the triangle of garden at the far end of Ann Street which was given to the Ann Street Society in 1973 by Caledonian Insurance, of which Raeburn was a director. Back on the main road, you are in a different world.

Turn right and cross the end of St Bernard's Crescent. On the opposite corner, the St Bernard's Education Centre was built as a school in 1874 by the Heriot's Trust. The characteristic Jacobean-style decoration above the windows derived from the original Heriot's Hospital in Lauriston.

Follow the road as it bends round into Dean Street. On

your right side are the rather less prepossessing backs of St Bernard Crescent punctuated by shops, cellars and the tiny Dean Bar in the basement. On the left, the octagonal building is the community hall of Stockbridge House, providing facilities for older people since 1975 when it was opened by the most famous member of their generation, the Queen Mother.

Pass the end of Cheyne Street and turn left through the gateposts into **Raeburn Street**, another of Edinburgh's hidden corners. Formerly known as Hermitage Place, this cobbled lane originally had gates at each end, supposedly because it once housed a nunnery. Its row of two-storied houses with a grander pedimented centrepiece looks like a doll's house version of Heriot Row.

Turn right into **Raeburn Place**, a lively shopping street that still retains some fresh food shops, including one of the best butchers in town. The old double villas are now rather lost behind the shop fronts.

Cross the road at the lights and continue along Raeburn Place. Turn left at Bert's Bar, a recreation of a traditional Scottish pub, into St Bernard's Row. No 1 on the right, now an architects office, may date back to the late eighteenth century, a relic of the original Stockbridge village. Further along on the right is Malta Terrace, a neat Georgian row with a bit of later infill, but unfortunately with no access to the river.

To reach the Water of Leith, return to Raeburn Place and continue along its extension, Deanhaugh Street. Turn left into Haugh Street. To the left the modern Veitch's Square replaces a rectangle of thatched cottages round a central green once frequented largely by widows and spinsters who took in washing.

Go through the gate onto the **Water of Leith Walkway** and turn left. Across the river the houses look as if at one time they were industrial workshops. Trees and shrubs grow in the parts of the river bed which are exposed unless the waters are in full spate. In season look out for the exotic Himalayan balsam with its purple flowers and seed pods which explode to the touch. It grows here in profusion. Ducks and drakes dabble at the water's edge and there is the occasional scent of a fox.

Follow the Walkway, then turn right to cross the Falshaw Bridge, built as a joint venture between the Town Council and the City Road Trust in 1877. On your left are Reid Terrace and Hugh Miller Place, the first two terraces of the Stockbridge Colonies built by a co-operative of artisans in the latter half of the nineteenth century (*See box, Walk 8*).

> **Reid Terrace** is named after Hugh Gilzean Reid, a journalist, Liberal MP, the first chairman of the co-operative and its moving spirit. **Hugh Miller** was a self-taught stonemason who wrote 'best-sellers' about the geology of the north east of Scotland. A deeply religious man and an early socialist, he was a patron of the Trust. Tragically he committed suicide, possibly because of his inability to reconcile his religious convictions with the scientific discoveries in which he played a part.

Passing the Colony Shop on your left, take the winding path up the hill to the right with good views of the Colonies. Ahead stands the huge red fortress or cathedral of

The Colonies

Glenogle Public Baths, built in 1897. The path emerges at the end of **Saxe-Coburg Place**. Started in 1821, with James Milne as architect, it was sadly never finished. Nonetheless it makes an attractive northern end-piece to the New Town.

Turn right and walk along Saxe-Coburg Place to the corner with Dean Park Lane. Facing you across the lane is Dean Bank House, one of the few remaining pre-nineteenth century houses with a large gothic window and pinnacles balancing spheres on the corners of the gables.

Turn right into **Dean Bank Lane**. The houses on the right have gardens sloping steeply down to the Water of Leith. Number 4 was formerly the Dean Bank Institution, founded in 1832 as a house of correction for homeless young women who had committed minor crimes.

The lane curves down to join Hamilton Place by the red sandstone Stockbridge Library. Follow Hamilton Place back to the bridge and the start of the walk.

WALK 8

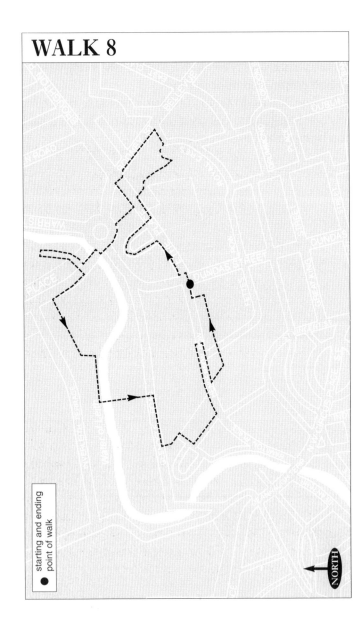

starting and ending
point of walk

NORTH

Walk 8
THE WORKING NEW TOWN
Canonmills and Silvermills

The walk explores the New Town's industrial past, from the mills from which the working villages took their names to the power station for the city's tramway system. Skirting the boundaries where the planned New Town merges with the later piecemeal development of the city, the walk provides a glimpse of the sheer diversity of architectural styles and the subtlety of social gradations that give the New Town its distinctive character.

Introduction

Even with the expansion of the New Town, the villages strung along the Water of Leith remained separate communities, proud of their traditions and heritage. Canonmills and Silvermills grew up round the industries that supplied the city—flourmills, tanneries, stonemasons' yards and blacksmiths' forges. It is only in the last thirty years that light industry at the foot of the hill has finally given way to the pressures of rising land values and city-centre living.

The coming of the railway provided a new impetus for

industry and changed the character of the north-eastern New Town. Built in 1842 to connect Edinburgh to its port at Leith, the line was taken up the hill through the Scotland Street tunnel. Although it adopted the most direct route to the terminus at Princes Street, at 1 in 27 the gradient was extremely steep.

In order to overcome this difficulty, outward trains were rolled down the hill under their own momentum, held in check by brake-vans. At Scotland Street Station, the locomotive was attached to continue the journey to Leith. On the return journey, the carriages were hauled up the hill on cables powered by stationary engines. With the opening of the alternative line to Leith via Abbeyhill in 1862, the Scotland Street line was relegated to mineral traffic. It finally closed in 1868.

Route

The starting point for the walk is the foot of **Dundas Street** at its intersection with Eyre Place. It can be reached by walking down Hanover Street and Dundas Street or by taking buses 23, 27 or 37 from the foot of the Mound. Ask for the last stop in Dundas Street.

Cross Dundas Street at the lights. A few yards up on the right is a late-twentieth century interpretation of New Town classicism in the pillared frontage of the former headquarters of the Life Association of Scotland. Built in 1990 by Reiach and Hall, the award-winning building is now part of the Royal Bank of Scotland, while its bronzed neighbour belongs to the TSB. Although the banks and some insurance companies retain their grand palaces higher up the hill, the industry of the edge of the New Town is now the business of computer centres and financial processing.

Cross **Eyre Place** and turn right along it. The name celebrates James Eyre, whose house and brewery were formerly in the centre of the crescent. The basements boast fine gardens.

Turn left to go round **Eyre Crescent**, whose heavy Victorian frontages awkwardly combine rectangular and hexagonal bay windows. Unlike the earlier New Town developments, these are clearly tenements, the 'main doors' opening onto tiny gardens and the windows of the 'stairs' to the upper floors clearly distinguished. The palace facades have been abandoned in favour of comfortable Victorian gentility. The central garden of the Crescent, formerly dominated by a church, is now sheltered housing.

On rejoining Eyre Place, turn left and then right down Logan Street to reach **George V Park**.

From 1860 this was the site of the **Royal Patent Gymnasium** promoted by John Cox, of Cox's Gelatine, as the healthy equivalent of a theme park. The star attractions were a giant rowing machine for 600 people, called the Great Sea Serpent, and an immense see-saw carrying up to 200 revellers 50 feet into the air. The Gymnasium was an immediate popular sensation. In the longer term, dependent as it was on large numbers of visitors for its effective operation, it could not cope with the vagaries of the Scottish weather and gradually fizzled out by 1880.

The ground was then used intermittently by **St Bernard's Football Club** until 'the Saints' moved to Powderhall to become one of Scotland's leading clubs. They won the Scottish Cup in 1895 by beating Renton 2-1 at Ibrox. The Saints returned to the Gymnasium site in 1902, by now relegated to the Second Division although continuing to attract strong local support. The Army requisitioned the ground during the First World War, treating it with scant respect.

At the end of the War it was reinstated as a football ground with the pitch now running east-west and a stand on the south side reached by a bridge from Royal Crescent. In the 1930s the club hit serious financial problems, resorting to devices such as using the ground as a greyhound track to keep afloat. It failed to survive the Second World War.

The ground was sold to the City Corporation for a George V Memorial Park, one of many open spaces so dedicated throughout Britain. It opened in 1950 with a playground, rose garden, putting green and tennis courts, but gradually fell into disrepair. In the mid-1980s, a playground was successfully promoted by the New Town Community Council. The Park now includes Scotland Yard Adventure Centre, belonging to the Scottish Adventure Playgrounds Association for Handicapped Children.

Go through the Park following the cobbled track to the left and keeping left at the roundabout to reach an area between two blocked-off tunnels. This is the site of the former Scotland Street Station. After the railway closed, the tunnels were used unsuccessfully for growing mushrooms. During the Second World War, they became an air-raid shelter for 1,250 railway staff and the control centre for Waverley Station. In 1948 a lecturer at Edinburgh University conducted atomic physics experiments in them, while the fungi growing on their walls were used as a source of penicillin. Today, the tunnels lie dank and abandoned, although the path and signs suggest that there may at one time have been plans to open the northern tunnel as a cycle track.

Cross the line of the tracks and take the flight of steps leading up the opposite bank. The path winds up through scrubby woodland to reach Sunnybank at the corner of Cornwallis Place.

Go along Cornwallis Place past the Bellevue Chapel to reach **Rodney Street**. Turn right and go up a few yards to look into **Bellevue Crescent** with the grandly classical St Mary's Church as its centrepiece. First devised in 1818 as part of the Second New Town, the Crescent missed the building boom, its northern half not being completed until 1884.

Retrace your steps and continue down busy Rodney Street past Canonmills Primary School, the British Legion's Elsie Clark Halls and a former warehouse now boldly proclaiming itself to be the Union advertising agency. The new housing running back to the tunnels reflects the continuing shift in the character of the area from industrial to residential.

Turn left down a few steps into the narrow atmospheric alley to rejoin Eyre Place. Cross the road, turning left past Smithie's pub, then thereafter right into **Canon Street**. On the corner, the former Canon Mill now houses the Leith Agency, one of Scotland's leading advertising agencies. Notice the curious kingfisher, wolf, cockerel, magpie and squirrel on the corners of the roof!

Just to the left is the site of **Canonmills Loch**. Two mill lades ran from Silvermills, one stream following approximately the line of Henderson Row, the other running below Fettes

Row and Royal Crescent. They met up again in a small loch just off Rodney Street. From the loch, a lade flowed into the Water of Leith to power the mills of Canonmills, built by David I for use by the vassals of the Canons of Holyrood. In medieval times, the vassals and the Incorporation of Baxters of the Canongate were required by law to use these mills and no other, thus providing a regular source of revenue for the Abbey. Industrial Canonmills later included flour and paper mills, tanneries and a distillery.

In 1783, after a bad harvest and resultant food shortages, a rumour spread throughout Edinburgh that Haig's whisky distillery in Canonmills was using oats and potatoes to ensure continued production. What became known as the Meal Mob of angry and hungry citizens attacked the factory which was defended by employees armed for the purpose.

The loch was about four feet deep, the haunt of fishermen and wild fowlers. After the Nor' Loch was drained, in winter Canonmills Loch became Edinburgh's official curling rink. The game involves sliding large granite stones across the ice to stop on a particular target. By the end of the eighteenth century, Canonmills was eclipsed by Duddingston Loch and, in 1847, the Loch was finally drained.

Go down Canon Street and cross Rodney Street at the traffic island. The tenements round Canonmills are simpler, albeit with elegant fans over windows and doors, and there is still some light industry and wholesaling business. Turn left, crossing Warriston Road and passing the clock in the middle of the road to cross **Canonmills Bridge**. In the eighteenth century there was a sedan chair stance at its northern end, with four carriers and four porters employed by the

Town Council. When not bearing sedan chairs and their occupants up the hill, the 'cadies' were expected to carry coal and bottles, using ropes and creels to help them tackle the steep climb.

Continue up **Inverleith Row** to **Warriston Crescent**. As the New Town expanded northwards, the outlying village of Canonmills, near but not too near the city, was considered an attractive place to live. Development started in 1806 to designs by Gillespie Graham, with Howard Place facing the main road north and elegant Warriston Crescent backing onto the Water of Leith. The Polish composer Fryderyk Chopin stayed at no 10 Warriston Crescent during a visit to Edinburgh in 1848. There is a traditional red telephone box preserved in the basement of no 9.

Return to Inverleith Row. On the corner, the Northern Bar with its fine Edwardian exterior used to be a ground-floor tenement with an older pub in the basement below. When the ground floor was converted the internal metal beams and columns were inserted to avoid the upper floors crashing down on the heads of the customers.

Cross at the lights to your left and turn right to continue up the hill, passing the computer centre of the major insurance company, Standard Life, built by Michael Laird & Partners in 1991. Outside stands a dramatic bronze sculpture by Gerald Laing called *Axis Mundi*, and a boulder commemorating Tanfield Hall.

Tanfield Hall was the meeting place of the first Free Church Assembly after the Disruption of 1843. 472 ministers of the Church of Scotland, supported by many lay elders, walked out of the General Assembly, then in session at St Andrew's and St George's Church in George Street. The walkout was in protest at the imposition of lay patronage in the appointment of ministers. Patronage, whereby the owner of the living, usually the local landlord, chose the minister, was against the Presbyterian principle that ministers must be appointed by the congregation and its elected elders.

By walking out on a point of principle, the ministers sacrificed their livings, their homes in the Church-owned manses and their position in society. They marched in procession down Dundas Street, watched by an admiring and wondering crowd to Tanfield Hall, hired in preparation for such an event. Lord Cockburn commented: 'The common sneers at the venality of our country, never just, are now absurd'.

With strong popular support, the Free Church prospered, almost displacing the Established Church in many areas. The majority of the Churches reunited in 1928, the Established Church having by then abandoned lay patronage, although the Free Church still remains strong in parts of the Highlands and Islands.

Across the road, no 8 **Howard Place** is the birthplace of Robert Louis Stevenson, who spent his early childhood in Canonmills, first here and then at no 1 Inverleith Terrace. He attended the local primary school. The damp and low-lying situation, however, did not suit his delicate health and the family soon moved up the hill to Heriot Row (see Walk 3).

Turn left down Inverleith Terrace Lane signposted to the Water of Leith Walkway. Alternatively, you may wish to continue about 100 yards up Inverleith Row to the Royal

Botanic Garden, which is well worth a visit. Highlights include the world's largest collection of rhododendrons, a magnificent nineteenth-century palm house, a newly laid-out Chinese garden, and the eighteenth-century Inverleith House which often displays temporary art exhibitions. There is also a cafe and a shop.

At the end of the lane, turn left onto Rocheid Path along the banks of the Water of Leith, with, on your right, a luxury housing development round the former St Colm's College. This was built in 1908 as a Free Church College for Lady Missionaries.

Ignore the first bridge over the river and continue for about 200 yards to a humpbacked rustic bridge which you cross to reach the Stockbridge Colonies.

The Colonies were an innovative experiment to provide housing for working men on the principles of a co-operative. Many of the early co-op members were in the construction trades and personally worked on the buildings. The design adopted is ingenious. The Colonies were built in terraces with one house on the lower floor and a second above, accessible by an outer stair from the other side of the building. Thus, each house had access to a private garden.

From 1867 to 1886, 32 Bell Place in the second street was the home of the manager of the co-operative, James Colville, and his family. Its fine balconies single it out.

Since the names refer to each block of houses rather than the streets, the addresses are confusing, low numbers being in one street and higher numbers in the next. Early policy was to name terraces after directors or supporters—Reid, Hugh Miller, Colville (*see Walk 7*). It

switched to picturesque names such as Avondale and
Balmoral when the chairman's name was proposed for a
street but failed to win a seconder!

At their peak in 1880, the Colonies housed over 2,000
people. 25 Collins Place was occupied by a family with
nine children. Briefly threatened by demolition for a proposed ring road, the Colonies were 'discovered' in the
1960s as an attractive place to live.

Go to the end of Bell Place, passing on your left Glenogle
House, the original house on the site, and turn right into
Glenogle Road. In passing the end of the Colonies, note
the sculptures representing the trades involved in the co-
op, on the ends of Kemp, Avondale, Teviotdale, and
Dunrobin Terraces.

Turn left just before the red chimney of Glenogle Baths to
take Gabriel's Steps up the bank on the opposite side of the
road to reach Saxe-Coburg Place. The steps follow the line of
Gabriel's Lane, a traditional route across the New Town,
from Mutrie's Hill (*see Walk 1*) to Stockbridge (*see Walk 8*).

At the top, turn right into Saxe-Coburg Street and follow
it as it bears left to pass the plain classical frontage of St
Bernard's Parish Church. It was built in 1813 as a chapel of
ease to spare the inhabitants of Stockbridge the long walk
up the hill to St Cuthbert's. It is still the local parish church.

At the end of Saxe-Coburg Street, turn left into
Henderson Row. A hundred yards further along on the left
is Edinburgh Academy. The first courtyard was built in 1823
by Gillespie Graham as the Deaf and Dumb Institution,
resulting in Gabriel's Steps being known as the Dumbie

Edinburgh Academy

Steps. The second is the original Edinburgh Academy building, designed by William Burn in the fashionable Greek-revival style. Built in 1822 as a rival to the High School, the Academy remains one of Edinburgh's leading independent schools (*see Walk 10*).

Cross the road and retrace your steps a little to turn left up **West Silvermills Lane**, another section of Gabriel's Lane. Although much altered, the house on the left predates the New Town. Follow the lane round to the left through modern housing to reach the dramatic statue of 'Horse Rider Eagle' by Eoghan Bridge.

Turn left and follow the lane round to pass the back of the chateau-style offices of the Scottish Life Assurance Company. The building incorporates the facade of the power station that drove the cable tram cars which ran up to Hanover Street. On the other side of the lane, Silvermills Court Business Centre continues the area's industrial tradition. The area owes its name to the mill for working silver and precious metal into coinage which was located here in the late Middle Ages.

Return to Henderson Row, turning left into Henderson Place. Look out for the two cable wheels on your left. Turn right to return to Dundas Street and the end of the walk.

Walk 9
TOP OF THE WALK

Broughton and Gayfield

This walk is a real mix of architecture and atmosphere as it explores the eastern edge of the New Town and looks for a lost square and a lost village. It starts by taking you past one of Edinburgh's most ironic juxtapositions—the elegance of Robert Adam set against the backdrop of the city's ugliest building. It continues through the streets and lanes of the old and once separate community of Broughton before reaching Gayfield. One of the earliest parts of the New Town to be developed, its building styles range from the monumental to the almost rural. The walk ends by recalling the city's most famous detective and its greatest contemporary sculptor.

Introduction

Until the eighteenth century the Barony and Burgh of Regality of Broughton, to give the area its full title, lay outside the city. It dispensed its own justice through its own courts and protected its own trades against competition. Immediate power was in the hands of the owner of the land rather than, as was the case of the Royal Burgh of Edinburgh, the

WALK 9

NORTH

● starting and ending point of walk

King directly. Given to the Canons of Holyrood Abbey by David I in 1128, the lands included for many centuries most of the villages and farms outside the city boundary, from the adjacent Canongate, to Corstorphine and Liberton close to the modern city boundary.

In the Middle Ages, the village of Broughton or Brochtoun was little more than a scattering of crofts with its centre to the north of the present-day Albany Street. Situated on the route between the Port of Leith and the Castle, the everyday lives of its inhabitants were occasionally interrupted by high military drama. The Scots army under General Leslie set up their headquarters in Broughton to stop Oliver Cromwell taking Edinburgh Castle. Defensive embankments were built at the city end of Broughton, Greenside and Calton, and a high bank was built down towards Leith, later to be converted into Leith Walk.

After the Reformation, the lands belonging to Holyrood Abbey eventually passed to the Earl of Roxburghe. He borrowed money from the Heriot's Trust which he could not repay and in 1636 the lands round the Canongate were sold to the City Council, while those round Broughton were taken up by the Heriot's Trustees. In the seventeenth century the village acquired a certain notoriety because of the number of neighbourhood witches. Probably in practice no more than eccentric old women who had fallen foul of their neighbours at a time when superstition was rife, they were shut up in Broughton gaol and tortured into a confession before receiving a summary trial and the sentence of being burned alive.

During most of the eighteenth century the village remained unchanged, separated by fields and rough ground from the city. It lost its unusual status after the 1745 Rebellion when heritable jurisdictions were abolished throughout Scotland. A few Edinburgh merchants built country houses in the vicinity and the lanes and field paths made a popular Sunday stroll for residents of the increasingly congested Old Town.

Much of Broughton took on its present complexion in the early nineteenth century. The first area to be developed was the land round Gayfield House, feued by the solicitor James Jollie as early as 1785. Hugh Cairncross, an assistant of Robert Adam, worked on the designs. Picardy Place, Forth Street and Broughton Place followed close behind. Today, Broughton remains a lively mix of grand and not so grand, having largely survived the threat of traffic plans and large-scale re-development.

Route

At the East End of Princes Street, cross to the statue of the Duke of Wellington in front of Register House.

> **Register House** was a key element of the Proposals for the New Town of 1752. Providing a new and fitting home for the national records, stored in damp basements in the Old Town, was becoming an urgent priority. It was one of the first major buildings in the New Town and Europe's first purpose built repository for archives. Its site took in the cottage known as 'Peace and Plenty' where residents of the Old Town used to stop for fruit or curds and cream on a country Sunday outing.

Work on Register House started in 1774 to a design by Robert Adam but stopped four years later due to a shortage of funds. It remained roofless for some years, earning the title of 'the most magnificent pigeon house in Europe'. It was finally completed in 1803.

With its modest entrance and elegant low facade topped by a discreet dome, Register House forms a fitting introduction to the New Town: gracious, refined, but not overly welcoming. The interior, with its huge fireplace adorned by a lion and a unicorn, and its galleried reading room under the dome, well repays a visit. Register House is open on weekdays and often has temporary exhibitions in the foyer, drawing on the wealth of its archives.

Turn right and then left to take the black and white slabbed path running up the side of Register House with the entrance to the **St James Centre** shopping mall on your right. Passing on your left a 'bridge of sighs' connecting two parts of Register House, you reach a platform over a dusty garden. The bulk of New St Andrews House looms, eerie in its emptiness. It was built for the Scottish Office in the 1960s but is now vacant following the diagnosis of sick building syndrome and the civil servants' move to Leith

This derelict space was once Moutrie's Hill, the covert of the wild boar. Because of its vantage point, prisoners were hung from its trees as an example to the citizens. In the eighteenth century there was an abortive attempt to grow mulberry trees on its slopes to provide food for the silkworms that would create the raw material for the nearby weaving community.

At the end of the eighteenth century a square of tall,

plain tenements was erected on the crest of the hill to a ground plan design by James Craig. St James's Square was demolished in 1965 to make room for the St James Centre complex, arguably the ugliest building in the city. As a final insult to the past, the path down the side of the present square has been called James Craig Walk. No such honour has yet been given to his 1960s successor.

Continue straight ahead. On your left a short row of tenements is all that remains of the St James Square where Robert Burns stayed in 1787. It is followed by the main bus station, not a great welcome for a city that likes to think of itself as a European capital. Buried in the bus station is the rural-looking Postillion pub.

Keep alongside the back entrance to the shopping centre to join Elder Street. When the pavement runs out, cross to the right hand side of the street and carry on down to **York Place**, even busier now that it carries some of the traffic diverted from Princes Street. Cross at the lights. York Place was at one time part of the Broughton Parks farm where the autumn All Hallow's Fair was held before it moved to Calton Hill. Developed as part of James Craig's original plan, it still retains an elegant townscape and well-proportioned houses.

Turn right and go along a few doors to no 32 with its carved plaque in the shape of a palette. This was the studio of Sir Henry Raeburn, possibly Scotland's greatest portrait painter (*see Walk 7*). He installed large windows with multiple shutters which could be adjusted depending on the light to take advantage of the north-facing aspect of the

St George's Chapel and part of manse

rear of the building. These windows feature in some of his portraits.

Retrace your steps and continue along York Place. Across the road, the 1930s shop-front hides the former St George's Chapel with its octagonal dome. It was built in 1797 by James Adam who also designed the castellated manse next door. Ahead on your left is the Doge's Palace of the National Portrait Gallery where some of Raeburn's finest works can be seen.

Turn right down the steep slope of **Dublin Street**. Cross Albany Street, with its pleasant two-storey houses with dormer windows. To your left, Abercromby Place sweeps away in a shallow curve while ahead are the gardens of Drummond Place.

Turn right into Dublin Street Lane North to reach **Broughton Market**, established in the 1840s as a fruit, vegetable and meat market. It cut a swathe through the west end of the old village, some of whose building stone was re-used in the adjacent walls. The market buildings now house garages and workshops.

Follow the lane round the end of Broughton Market, then left into **Barony Street** and then left again into Old Broughton. Once the centre of the village, Old Broughton and, round the corner, New Broughton, is little more than Jenner's Garage, modern flats and a traditional drying green.

Returning to Barony Street via Barony Place, cross and turn right. Just past the turn up **Albany Lane** lies the dour Glassite meeting house, built in 1835 for the sect founded by John Glas in 1730.

The **Glassites** strove to go back to the primitive Church, conducting simple unemotional services at which the whole Bible was read over a period. These were followed by communal 'Feasts' of kail soup in an upstairs dining room, earning them the nickname of the 'Kailites'. The last Glassite elder was appointed in 1967. Noted for a coldly intellectual approach to religion, the severe building reflects their austere beliefs. Its sooty frontage is a reminder of what the New Town looked like in the era before stone cleaning and smokeless fuel. The Church is now the meeting place of the Architectural Heritage Trust.

Turn up Albany Lane and then left along Albany Street Lane. The mulberry-coloured mews conversion with its hidden entrance through a gate in Albany Lane is now an architect's office. Albany Street Lane leads you into the heart of **Broughton Street**, a bustling thoroughfare of pubs, second-hand furniture emporia, food shops and smart cafe bars, a sure sign that the area is on the way up. Across the road, the Barony Bar has a particularly attractive frontage, with a bell suggesting a previous name.

Turn left down Broughton Street, whose curves follow the route of an old country road, unlike the geometric lines of the New Town proper. Cross Barony Street, lined with plain high tenements without basements which, despite their utilitarian look, date back to 1830. Each row ends in an almost circular turret facing on to Broughton Street. At the foot of the street is a large, neo-Norman church, designed by Rowand Anderson in 1872.

This, the former Catholic Apostolic Church, contains murals painted in the 1890s by the Dublin-born **Phoebe Traquair**. Angelic choirs, the Wise and Foolish Virgins, Saints, Elders, and Christ in Glory adorn the interior in a profusion of rich colours and gold leaf. The redundant building has recently been purchased by the Mansfield Traquair Trust which was formed to save its treasures. While the basement will become the headquarters of the Scottish Council of Voluntary Organisations, the nave and apse will be used as a meeting and performance space, with the murals restored to their former glory.

Cross the busy Broughton Street at the pedestrian lights, and return up the hill. Wall painting moves from the religious to the secular. Above is a fine example of a gold pestle and mortar, the sign of the chemist in an era when many people could not read. On your left is a brightly painted street scene and, at the corner of **Broughton Place**, a surreal mural with echoes of Dali, framed in a blocked-up window.

Cross and turn left into Broughton Place. Opposite is a miniature version of a Heriot Row terrace with its central pedimented facade and basements whose stonework has been cleft to give the effect of a natural rock face. This early New Town development, feued in 1807, is neatly closed off by the Doric portico of the former Broughton Place Church, occasionally used as a Festival Fringe venue. Built in 1785 by the Rose Street Secessionist Church which had become too small for its congregation, it was known as John Brown's chapel after the popularity of its second minister.

The Secessionists were one of many groups which split from the Church of Scotland in the seventeenth and eoghteenth centuries over its relations with the state. Split often turned into splinter, with the Rose Street Church congregation breaking off from the parent body over the disputed appointment of a minister. The classical style chosen for the church is probably a reaction to the choice of gothic by the Episcopalians and Catholics.

Crossing Hart Street, follow the road round to the right of the Church into **Union Street**. Before turning first left into **Gayfield Street**, go up the steep hill a few yards past the church hall, an extremely domestic-looking appendage to its classical neighbour. Unusually, the houses opposite have front gardens, one planted with a crop of potatoes. A

Gayfield House

few yards further up on the left is the Edinburgh Printmakers Workshop and gallery with its hanging signs and bright red chimney suggesting that at one time it had a more basic purpose as a communal wash house or 'steamie'.

Carry on along Gayfield Street. Look down Gayfield Street Lane on your left to see the overhanging apse of Broughton Place Church and, opposite, the balcony access of the houses in Shaw's Square.

Turn left down **Gayfield Square**, at this point in practice a street. At its head stands Gayfield House.

Gayfield House was built in 1763 by Charles and William Butter the Deacon of Wrights and first occupied by David 6th Earl of Leven. In 1874, Gayfield House became the base of the New Veterinary College. Following a disagreement with his Board of Management, William Williams, Principal of the Dick Veterinary School, the city's senior veterinary training school, took 40 of its 49 pupils with him when he set up the rival establishment. It survived until 1904, when the house was bought by a manure merchant, William Cockburn. Gayfield House now lies at the very edge of the New Town, stranded in a sea of garages, warehouses and workshops. They occupy the ground which Playfair's grand scheme never reached.

A few steps down on the left take you into one of the city's hidden corners. **Shaw's Square** was built in the 1870s as housing for the construction workers employed on the Bellevue development.

Return to Gayfield Square proper, a mass of crocuses in early Spring. Turn left along the bottom of the square and keep straight ahead to enter Gayfield Place Lane, which backs onto a bleak office block. In the corner, a small gap site, currently being advertised for residential development, is a reminder that the New Town is not even now complete!

Follow the Lane round to **Leith Walk**, turning right at the top of the steps. The Christadelphian Church occupies one of the tall Venetian-style tenements on your right. Across the Walk the very grand buildings sweeping round the corners into Montgomery Street and London Road were designed to form an imposing entrance to Playfair's largely abortive scheme (*see Walk 10*).

As you go up Leith Walk you have the best view of Gayfield Square with its imposing tenements and early villas. Along the top of the square are benches, like surfboards balanced on footballs, perfectly functional despite their impractical appearance. These are part of the improvements to Leith Walk, which also include the reinstatement of some of the trees which gave **Elm Row**, opposite, its name. Gourmets will want to cross over to 19 Elm Row to pay homage to Valvona and Crolla's, Edinburgh's much-loved Italian delicatessen.

An ornate clock in the middle of the road marks the London Road turning, with views up to Calton Hill. Further up Leith Walk, one of the well-restored early tenements of **Baxter's Place** was the home of Robert Stevenson, lighthouse engineer and grandfather to Robert Louis Stevenson. Opposite, the construction of the Playhouse Theatre is ingenious. The auditorium slopes down the hill so that the stalls are downstairs and there is only a short climb to the balcony. The theatre stages long-running West End musicals and pop concerts. The adjacent Tudor-style church was built for yet another of the city's nineteenth-century sects, under the patronage of Lady Glenorchy. Its facade is to be incorporated into an as yet unspecified building development.

Picardy Place recalls the time when a community of weavers from St Quentin in the Picardy region of France settled in the area to escape persecution for their Protestant beliefs. At the time, the Board of Manufactures, Scotland's original economic development agency, was keen to attract skilled weavers from overseas to instruct local workers in linen manufacture. For a time, the weavers tried to establish a silk industry but after this enterprise failed, the land was laid out for streets and housing in the early years of the nineteenth century.

Follow the road round into Picardy Place. In a sea of shrubbery and parking spaces stands a statue of Sherlock Holmes. It was donated by the Federation of Master Builders to commemorate their centenary in 1991 and unveiled by the President of the Royal College of Surgeons, an unusual combination of professions. They were honouring the birth of Sir Arthur Conan Doyle in 1859 in a house, since demolished, at 11 Picardy Place. The creator of the immortal detective was brought up here, one of the seven children of an alcoholic civil servant. Robert Burn, the architect of Picardy Place, ran a drawing academy in the house with the bow window at the corner of Broughton Street.

Continue round to the traffic lights. Ahead is St Paul's and St George's Episcopal Church, built by Archibald Eliot in 1816 in the style of a college chapel. Its elegance is rather cramped by its 1960s neighbour.

Cross York Place. To the left is St Mary's Roman Catholic Cathedral, a very modest edifice compared with its Anglican namesake in the West End. Although the facade of the Cathedral is inherited from a chapel of 1813 by Gillespie Graham, the interior was remodelled in the 1890s and again in the 1930s.

In front of the cathedral is 'Manuscript of Monte Cassino', created by Scotland's leading sculptor, Sir Eduardo Paolozzi. The sculptural ensemble is made up of a giant foot, ankle and hand, the latter holding a pair of mating locusts, a small machine and what could be a flattened cat! The Latin inscriptions may give a clue to the underlying inspiration.

Continue round the corner into Leith Street, passing the back door of John Lewis's department store. This extension to the St James Centre at least creates some interest at street level. As you approach North Bridge and the end of the walk, the high tenements opposite give some idea of the narrow canyon which was once the eastern approach to the city.

WALK 10

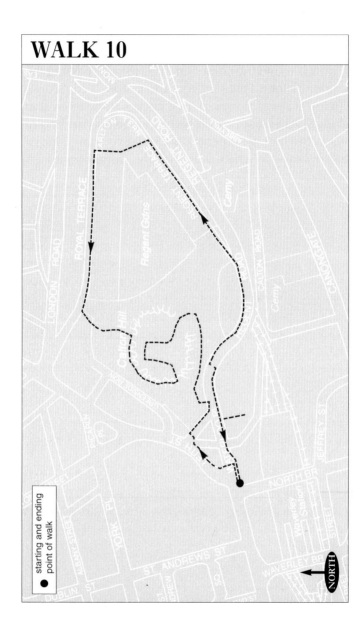

starting and ending
point of walk

NORTH

Walk 10
ATHENS OF THE NORTH

Calton Hill

After looking for traces of the old village of Calton, you visit a cemetery and pass a might-have-been Parliament before taking a stroll along the elegant terraces which follow the contours of the hill. A stiff climb is rewarded by views over the city and the chance to explore the curious monuments on its crown before returning over a bridge which cost the Council as much as planning the First New Town.

Introduction

Edinburgh, the Athens of the North, boasts more than one Acropolis. While the Castle rock was the key military stronghold, the ambition in the more peaceful eighteenth century was to create a monumental showpiece on Calton Hill true to the spirit of the Athenian Acropolis.

Until the end of the eighteenth century Calton Hill lay outside the city, separated from both the Old and New Towns by steep valleys. This wild and unfrequented spot met the very different needs of an astronomical observatory and a prison. In 1791 the Old Observatory was erected on the top of the hill, and the Bridewell or House of Correction, a semicircular building by Robert Adam, was constructed to the south. Proposals for an improved access road were abandoned as prohibitively expensive.

The problem of access became acute in 1815 when the decision was taken to erect a new gaol adjoining the Bridewell to house long-term prisoners from all over Scotland. Possible sites in the Old Town and at the east end of Princes Street were rejected on the grounds that their narrow lanes were inconvenient and a security risk. It was decided, therefore, to extend Princes Street by taking it on a bridge across the intervening ravine of Low Calton and up and along the side of Calton Hill. The row of houses blocking the east end of Princes Street was to be demolished.

The original proposal for Regent Bridge was modelled on Pulteney Bridge in Bath with its enclosed sides of shops. Robert Stevenson, the engineer appointed, suggested that the sides of Regent Bridge should be open so that those passing over could admire the views. Finance proved a continuing difficulty; in the end the cost of the scheme to the Council was greater than that of laying out the first New Town. Some of the graves of Old Calton Cemetery had to be moved to a new burial ground further up the hill as they were in the path of the new road, which was finally completed in 1821.

Improved access opened up Calton Hill for development. In 1812, the owners of the land, Mr Allan of Hillside, the Trinity Trust and the Heriot's Trust, held a competition to plan not only Calton Hill but also a large area to the north between Edinburgh and Leith. When no clear winner emerged, the developers asked a number of leading architects to report on the designs and appointed two judges to assess their reports. All this was to no avail. None of the plans was entirely to their liking.

The judges did, however, commend a paper submitted by William Stark, who took ill and died before being able to submit his full report as one of the commissioned architects. He argued that any plan should aim to take maximum advantage of the Hill's views and prospects rather than adopt an orderly geometric layout. While the latter might look good on paper, it would not work on the ground. Roads should follow the contours of the hill and trees should be retained or planted to set off the buildings.

Finally, William Playfair was appointed to draw up plans in accordance with Stark's principles which 'had given universal satisfaction'. He complied enthusiastically, proposing to ring the Hill with a series of terraces while retaining the hilltop as open space. To the north he envisaged a wide crescent followed by squares of cheaper housing.

Playfair justified the relatively prodigal use of land by the need to compete with the more established developments going up to the west of the First New Town; the gardens, views and open outlook would be the major selling points of his scheme. In the end, only the terraces along the hill, and a few streets near Hillside Crescent off London Road, were built of what would have been the largest New Town of all. East End lost out to West End. Meanwhile, the hill was acquiring its strange crop of monuments on top and the new classical Royal High School on its flank.

In 1936 Calton Hill gained a new role as the seat of Government in Scotland when the prisons were replaced by the monumental St Andrew's House. In 1979, the Hill won symbolic significance as the designated site of the Scottish Assembly. When at last, twenty years later, Scots voted decisively for their own Parliament, Calton Hill was rejected in favour of a new building beside Holyrood Palace. St Andrew's House, however, will be the seat of the Scottish Executive, ensuring the Hill's continuing role at the nation's heart.

Route

From the Princes Street end of North Bridge, turn right past the classical facade of the former General Post Office built on the site occupied in the early days of the New Town by the Royal Theatre.

Cross at the lights to the top of Leith Street and follow the canyon down. Across the road is the New Town's and probably Edinburgh's greatest planning disaster, the enormous bulk of the St James Centre, a shopping mall, hotel and now empty government office block. It looms large in the views throughout this walk. Ahead, Greenside, the gap site, soon to be a multiplex cinema, was once the city's tournament ground and racecourse. It is said that Mary, Queen of Scots first fell in love with the Earl of Bothwell when she watched him cut a dash as he galloped down Calton Hill into the arena.

Take the steps down into Calton Road to obtain a view of Regent Bridge from below. It was opened in 1819 by Leopold, later King of the Belgiums and Queen Victoria's 'dear uncle'. Its porticoes and columns celebrate the victory over Napoleon. Through the bridge there is access to a footbridge leading to the east end of platform 1 in Waverley Station, one way to start the walk straight from the train.

Cross Calton Road and turn right up Calton Hill, a pleasant cobbled route winding steeply up from Leith Street to Regent Road. There is a path just above the left side of the road, giving an easier ascent. Mrs Agnes Maclehose, Burns's 'Clarinda', lived in no 14 from 1800 to 1841. Daniel and George Wilson were born at no 5. Daniel became President of Toronto University while George was briefly the world's first Professor of Technology at Edinburgh University in 1850.

At the top, Rock House is famous in the annals of photography as the studio of the pioneer, David Octavius Hill. For over a century thereafter it continued as a photographic studio, belonging successively to Archibald Burns, Alexander Adam Inglis and Francis Caird Inglis.

On reaching Regent Road look to your right for a spectacular view along the length of Princes Street, framed by the spires and towers of the Balmoral Hotel, Scott Monument, St John's Church and St Mary's Cathedral.

Cross the road and bear right to enter Calton Old Cemetery. The elegant classical arcades processing up the hill are in fact the retaining walls for the cemeteries whose taller tombs peek over the walls. At the top of the steps, look back for a view of Rock House and the cluster of monuments on top of Calton Hill. Ahead is the large obelisk to the Scottish political martyrs, including Thomas Muir, who were transported to Botany Bay in Australia for supporting democracy at the time of the French Revolution. Their fate may have inspired Burns to write *Scots Wha' Hae*. The Complete Suffrage Association erected the monument in 1844 during the next period of revolutionary fervour.

On the right up a short flight of steps is the cylindrical monument to David Hume, the philosopher and historian. It was modelled by Robert Adam on the mausoleum of Theodoric in Ravenna. Next to it, somewhat unexpectedly, is a statue of Abraham Lincoln, in memory of the Scottish-American soldiers who fell in the American Civil War. To the left of the martyr's obelisk across the wall is the castellated folly of the Governor's House, all that remains of Calton Gaol. The Gaol was an eighteenth-century vision of a medieval castle, with towers, battlements and turrets.

Returning to Regent Road, turn right up the hill. St Andrew's House has none of the inappropriate frivolity of the Gaol it replaced. It exudes authority as a seat of Government should. Beyond, on the left, stands the former Royal High School.

The **Royal High School** building originated with the proposal in 1822, made by a Committee of Subscribers including Lord Cockburn and Walter Scott, to establish a second school in the expanding city. On the basis that it would be a satellite of the existing High School in the Old

Town, the Council agreed to build the school. A site at Canonmills was chosen and William Burn appointed architect. When his plans came in over budget as usual, another architect, Thomas Hamilton, was brought in.

Some members of the Town Council started to have cold feet, doubting the viability of two grammar schools in the city and arguing that Canonmills was too far from the Old Town. The proposed fees to recoup costs would create 'a separation between the different classes of the community, thereby destroying what has hitherto been one of the proudest characteristics of the Scottish system of education'.

The Council decided that that the city should have one school in a new central location. Princes Street Gardens were rejected, as the likely objections to building there were by now well known. It was outbid by the Royal Bank of Scotland for Robert Dundas's house in St Andrew Square. Eventually, in 1825, the Calton Hill site was chosen and Thomas Hamilton commissioned to produce a design.

Having failed to persuade the Council to honour its original commitment, the subscribers decided to go it alone and the Edinburgh Academy, designed by William Burn, opened in Canonmills in 1824 (*see Walk 8*). With its imposing Doric porticoes, the new High School, opened five years after the Academy, remains a key monument of the Scottish Greek revival. In 1968 the school was moved to Barnton, ironically again in search of a more socially exclusive catchment area!

In 1979 the High School building was adopted as the seat of the proposed Scottish Assembly. While showing a majority for an assembly, a referendum failed to deliver the required 40% of all voters in favour. Scotland had to wait 17 years for another opportunity. Throughout the intervening years, a group of staunch supporters of Scotland's aspirations to self-government maintained a Vigil for the Scottish Parliament on the triangle of ground outside the gates, in full view of the Scottish Office. A second referendum in 1997 was resoundingly in favour of devolution. Now deemed too small to house the Parliament, the future of the High School building is uncertain.

Follow the road as it bends round the Hill with magnificent views over the Old Town and Arthur's Seat. The cranes for the new Holyrood Parliament building will soon make their presence felt. Ahead, another cylindrical monument on a mound commemorates the poet, Robert Burns.

Cross the road and take Regent Terrace, the inconspicuous fork to the left. It soon opens out to a long and handsome terrace of houses: no 3 is the United States Consulate. Just before the terrace turns round the end of the hill, turn left into the picturesque Carlton Terrace Lane, lined with low cottages. This emerges into the even grander Royal Terrace, the longest in the New Town.

Turn left along Royal Terrace, once known as Whisky Row because of the number of wine and spirit merchants who lived here. They chose Royal Terrace, it was said, because they could keep a look out for their ships approaching Leith Harbour from their front windows. A quiet neighbourhood, less fashionable than the West End, although no less grand in design or aspect, Calton Hill proved particularly attractive to businessmen and retired East India Company officials. Alexander Gray, of Grays of George Street, the ironmongers, lived at no 4 and John Bartholomew, the mapmaker, at no 32. Helen Bannerman, the author of *Little Black Sambo,* was born at no 35, the house of her grandfather, Alexander Cowan, a paper manufacturer who had twenty children by two wives.

Many of the houses are now hotels, while the Danish Consulate shares no 4 with the Scottish Chamber Orchestra. Opposite the Terrace public gardens drop down to Playfair's London Road and Hillside Crescent. At the end, surrounded by trees, stands Greenside Church, built by Gillespie Graham in 1835.

Take the wide, stepped path leading forward up the hill behind the church. When it finally forks, take a sharp left turn to zigzag steeply up the hill towards the classical New Observatory. This building was designed by Playfair in 1818 for the Astronomical Institution, whose President was his uncle, John Playfair, Professor of Natural Philosophy at the University. The Observatory now houses the Edinburgh Experience, a multi-media journey round the City.

Take the path to the right round the observatories with spectacular views over the city, the Forth in the distance and the St James Centre all too prominent in the foreground. At the far side is the Old Observatory, built in 1776 for Thomas Short, the optician-astronomer, with support from the City and the University. James Craig, its designer, dressed it up as a medieval fortress to match Adam's Calton Gaol.

Return to the front of the Observatory, past the monument which Playfair built in gratitude to his uncle at the south east corner. Cut across to the National Monument, the apparently ruined but in fact merely incomplete replica of the Parthenon in Athens.

The National Monument

The National Monument was built by public subscription as a memorial to soldiers killed in the Napoleonic Wars and as a job-creation project for the unemployed. A subscription of £42,000 was called for in 1822 by a committee including Lord Cockburn and Sir Walter Scott. No more than half the money was ever raised. Work started in 1826, with Playfair again in charge. He wisely kept half an eye on producing a spectacular ruin, should the funds run out, as indeed they did in 1829. Although the building is often described as 'Scotland's Disgrace', it could have been worse—a full complement of pillars, all six feet high!

Go round to the right of the National Monument and take the track forwards, cutting across the grass to a small beehive cairn. This is a monument to the Vigil for a Scottish Parliament, incorporating a cobblestone thrown during the Paris riots of 1968 and a stone from the cottage which Robert Burns shared with Jean Armour. The quotations from supporters sum up Scotland's struggle for self-determination.

Return to the Nelson Memorial, the tower resembling an upturned telescope. Over the doorway is Nelson's crest and a model of the stern of the French flagship he captured. A white ball is dropped on the mast above at precisely one o'clock. This was originally a visual time check for ships in Leith Harbour, while the one o'clock gun, still fired every day from the Castle, gave the audible equivalent. Built in 1807 the house below was designed to accommodate disabled seamen but soon took on a less worthy role as a refreshment stall! The tower is open to the public, with fine views from the top. Just past the Monument, a cannon from the Crimean War points straight down Princes Street.

Follow the path forward towards the circular temple, another monument by Playfair commemorating Dugald Stewart, Professor of Moral Philosophy at the University.

Dugald Stewart's Monument

Although not now so well remembered as Adam Smith or David Hume, Dugald Stewart was an inspiring teacher who exercised great influence over intellectual life in Enlightenment Edinburgh.

Fork left down the hill on a path interspersed by flights of steps. Turn left after the first flight. Near the foot is one of Edinburgh's odder monuments, 'To Saint Wolodymyr the Great, Ruler of Ukraine, to commemorate a thousand years of Christianity in Ukraine, erected by Ukrainians in Scotland'.

Turn right onto Regent Road and cross Regent Bridge. As intended, the high arches permit views across to the Old Town and out to Leith and the Firth of Forth. Below is the sign for St Ninian's Row, the main street of old Calton village, now long gone. Soon you are back at North Bridge and the start of the walk.